Also by Brian Ray Gross

The Christmas Village
All Ye Faithful: A Christmas Village Story

Half the Man
I Used to Be

My Yearlong Journey to Stronger
Faith and Better Health

Brian Ray Gross

iUniverse LLC
Bloomington

HALF THE MAN I USED TO BE
MY YEARLONG JOURNEY TO STRONGER
FAITH AND BETTER HEALTH

iUniverse books may be ordered through booksellers or by contacting:

iUniverse LLC
1663 Liberty Drive
Bloomington, IN 47403
www.iuniverse.com
1-800-Authors (1-800-288-4677)

ISBN: 978-1-4917-3158-1 (sc)
ISBN: 978-1-4917-3218-2 (hc)
ISBN: 978-1-4917-3217-5 (e)

Library of Congress Control Number: 2014908168

Printed in the United States of America.

iUniverse rev. date: 05/09/2014

Contents

For Kristy, Brayden, Laura-Rae, and Spencer

You guys are my earthly inspiration; you are the reason I do what I do.

Acknowledgments

Most often when we achieve something in life, we don't accomplish it all by our lonesome. Usually, there are people who have contributed in some way to help us get where we are, whether it be by making sacrifices to help, lending an ear or financial support, or providing any other type of assistance. We all have our support group and I am no exception to this principle. The question is, though, where do I start?

Kristy—Words can't express how much your support means to me. I have never met anyone as forgiving, understanding, compassionate, and determined as you. When I first told you what I was facing, you never batted an eye and your never-quit attitude kicked in. If you ever doubted I would be successful, it never showed. We have been through a lot together and you have been crucial in helping me become the man I am today. In my eyes, you are the perfect spouse, partner, mother, and role model. I love everything about you, especially the fact that you support my hair-brained ideas and make me believe they can be successful.

Brayden, Laura-Rae, and Spencer—I always wanted to have three kids and I could not have asked for three better than you guys. You each have brought different types of joy to my life. Brayden, just as couples have starter homes, you were our starter child. I apologize for learning how to be a father on you; I know there were times you got the short end of the stick. But you teach me something new every day, and you never fail to entertain. Laura-Rae, every time I look into your precious blue eyes, I know I am in for a world of trouble as you get older. For now, though, I can take solace in the fact that you are wise beyond your years and your matter-of-fact demeanor is refreshing. Spencer, from one baby boy to another, you truly are the best surprise a guy could ever get. I can't even imagine what life would be like without you around and I don't even want to try. I promise to be the best father I can be. Daddy loves you guys!

Dad and Mom—In my opinion, you guys are the greatest earthly parents a child could possibly have. You have always been there for me, and even though I have let you down a few times, you have never let me down. You have been perfect role models for what parents should be, and I strive to emulate the example you set for me. Words can't express how much I truly appreciate all you have done for me throughout the years, but I can say I love both of you more and more each day.

Mammaw—It is my firm belief there has never lived a sweeter, more godly woman than you. Your sense of humor and ability to see the best in bad situations always brings comfort to anyone near you. Watching you with Pappaw as I was growing up was a special experience and I treasure those memories greatly. I don't get to see you as often as I would like, but please know that I love you tremendously.

Tonya and Jimmy—Tonya, you have been the best big sister a guy could ask for. You have been a sounding board for my writing ideas and have always been quick to help out when it comes to editing and revising. Your desire to achieve despite your circumstances has always inspired me and motivated me. Jimmy, your expertise and advice on this project have been immeasurable. Without your help during the editing and revising phase, I surely would have been lost. Your support and willingness to help are greatly appreciated. I love you both.

Artie, Greg, Danielle, and Patty—Artie, I have always looked up to you and been amazed how positive you remain no matter the situation. I admire that about you because I don't have that ability. Your faith is absolute and you truly are an instrument of God. Greg, there were times during our teenage years when we didn't get along so well. I guess that is pretty common. But all those times we fought and quarreled back then shaped the relationship we have today, and I wouldn't trade that for anything. Your perseverance and determination cannot be equaled. Dad has always said you remind him of himself when he was growing up, and I never could see that when we were young. I see it now and I know what he means. Danielle and Patty, you gals are more than sisters-in-law, you are sisters. You have stood by these crazy guys through thick and thin, and what you add to our family cannot be replaced. I love all you guys.

Tommy and Sandi—You have raised two wonderful girls, and I am grateful to have the privilege of sharing my life with one of them. Like many in-laws, we experienced some growing pains when we were first getting to know each other, but once we crossed over those speed bumps, our relationship blossomed. I am thankful for your love and support, and I want you to know I love both of you.

Kendra and Jonathan—Kendra, we have known each other and been friends long before we became family. You have always been a great sister to Kristy, and you are a great aunt to our kids. Your support of me over the years has been unconditional and unwavering. Jonathan, I have enjoyed getting to know you over the last several years. Your easy-going demeanor and ability to go with the flow is amazing. I am glad to call you guys my sister and brother. I love you both.

John and Ruthie—Divine guidance was at play when I was assigned to do my student teaching under John in 2003. Little did I know then that you guys would become such an integral part of my life and become a part of the family. You are the perfect godparents to our children, and you have come through in a pinch for us countless times. Both of you are guiding lights for the world to follow. I love you guys.

To all my nieces and nephews, you have provided me with great joy over the years, and I have cherished being your uncle. Many of you have already blossomed into magnificent young men and women who contribute greatly to society. Those who haven't yet reached that point, I can see the groundwork being laid for productive futures for all of you. You are our future, and I can only believe that future to be bright if you guys are leading the way. I love you all.

Dr. Carrie Connett—When I first met you, you had the difficult task of telling me I was far from healthy. I mistook your compassion for pity and resented it. After getting to know you, I have realized the error of my ways and cannot begin to thank you enough for the way you have handled my treatment. Your concern for my health, my future, and my family has been a driving force in successfully changing my life for the better. I respect the fact you were up-front with me about what I was facing and for being supportive the entire time. I don't know how I can ever thank you enough.

Jaclyn—Thanks for your tireless work on my cover photo. You did an amazing job, especially considering I'm not easiest subject for a photo shoot.

To the countless friends, co-workers, fellow congregants, and all who have offered kind words, support, and concern for my situation and my progress, I sincerely thank you. The interest you have taken in my health has been overwhelming and has reinforced in me when a man has friends, he most certainly is not a failure.

To everyone at iUniverse who had a hand in the publishing process, your expertise and assistance have been invaluable to this project, and I sincerely appreciate all the work and time you dedicated to making a dream come true.

Above all, though, I would like to thank Jesus Christ, my Lord and Savior, for taking my sins and the sins of all us upon Himself, and in so doing, allowing us to live through His grace so that we can share an eternal home together someday. There have been too many times in my life that I have turned away from Him and His guidance, but if I have learned anything over the last fifteen months, it is that He never gives up on us, and if we just listen to Him, He has a plan for all of us. I am thankful His hand guided me throughout the writing process and that even in the darkest of days, the Son shone through.

It is my hope the Lord uses my experience as an example to others and that anyone who reads this and is experiencing something similar can realize it is never too late to change, there is still hope, and there is light at the end of the tunnel. Thanks to all who shared in this experience with me and may God truly bless you all!

Brian Ray Gross
January 2014

Introduction

All humans have weaknesses. Even mythical warriors and super-heroes have a weakness. The Greek warrior Achilles was invincible to mortal blades, unless he was struck in the heel. Superman can't be harmed, except when he is in the presence of Kryptonite. We are all susceptible to something.

My Kryptonite is food, which creates an interesting paradox. Food is intended to strengthen us, nourish us, sustain us. Yet when we consume too much, we become weakened by it, and in this weakness, we cannot be the people God intends for us to be.

The Bible is full of tales of people who gave in to their weaknesses. Eve was tempted by the fruit in the Garden of Eden, and Adam, in an effort to please his mate, yielded to her judgment to partake of the forbidden fruit. David, a man after God's own heart, fell victim to lust, which led to adultery, deceit, and murder. Peter, perhaps the most passionate follower of Christ, denied Jesus three times and fled just before the Crucifixion. Yet, even after the Fall, God used Adam and Eve to sire humanity. Even after the sins they committed, God used the lineage of David and Bathsheba to produce the Savior. And even after turning his back on Jesus, God used Peter to proclaim and spread the Word in order to establish the Church. The Bible is full of tales of weakness, but it's also full of tales of redemption.

But we can't live without food. We must have it, and therein lies the problem. What do we do when our weakness is a necessity? From a purely physical aspect, the body can function at a premium level without drugs, alcohol, nicotine, sex, or any number of weaknesses people struggle with. The mind may tell the body those things are necessary, but they aren't. Food, however, is. You can't go cold turkey when it comes to eating. You can't go through a twelve-step program that allows you to never eat again. So, what can you do?

I faced this question directly in October 2012. I found out I was diabetic and my liver was failing. I was at my weakest point, and I had a choice to make. I could either continue to let the weakness dictate the rest of my life, or I could seek the strength to overcome. I chose the latter, and the kind of strength I needed could only come from one place: God.

I truly believe that by seeking His divine guidance, God has worked a miracle in my life. A few months into my lifestyle change, I felt a pressing need to tell others about how my life was being transformed. For the first time, I heard God's call, and it was telling me to bear witness to others in need. At that point, I began to consider the possibility of writing a book. I was encouraged by the results I had seen in such a short time, and I wanted to share my success with others.

I know how hard it is to lose weight. I know how easy it is to turn to food for comfort. I've been there; I've lived most of my life there and now that my life has changed, I never want to go back there. As long as I let God stay in the driver's seat, I won't.

If you can identify with this feeling, I want you to know, there is hope for you. It's not too late to regain the life you desire. If I can make changes, anybody can. It won't be easy. As a matter of fact, there will probably be times when you want to give up. But you aren't in this alone. You have people who care about you, who depend on you, who need you. And you have a Creator who made you in His image, and He wants the best for you. You can do this and when you do, you'll be glad you did.

Chapter 1

The Man-Mogram

"When pride comes, then comes disgrace;
but with humility comes wisdom."
Proverbs 11:2, *New International Version*

"Humiliation is the beginning of sanctification."
John Donne

Randy Travis sang in the classic country song "1982," "They say hindsight's 20/20 but I'm nearly going blind." When you think about it, that makes a lot of sense. Looking back on things, we can see them clearly but often if it is unpleasant, we choose to still not see it for what it is. Most of us have been through something we would rather not look back on with the clarity that time and distance give us so we choose to remember it the way that makes us feel the most comfortable. This, of course, is usually not a great idea.

My eye-opener came in the spring of 2012, and looking back, I should have recognized it for that instead of treating it as no big deal. I am usually pretty good at dealing with things and accepting difficulties that life throws my way. But we all have times when, in retrospect, we would have done things differently. I believe the Lord was trying to tell me something that spring, but I chose to look at it blindly instead of realistically, and several months later my whole world almost came crashing down on me. It went a little something like this.

One day when I was coming home from educating the youth at the juvenile detention facility where I teach, I noticed the seatbelt was rubbing across my right nipple and it was rather painful. I thought maybe one of my three rambunctious kids had hit me there by accident and left a bruise in that sensitive area. When I got home and started feeling around, I discovered a knot right under the skin by the nipple. Needless to say, I freaked out. The knot wasn't excruciating but it was painful and uncomfortable to touch. So I did what any guy who loves and respects his wife utterly and completely would do: I didn't tell her about it for nearly a month. I figured it would clear up sooner or later.

Naturally, it didn't happen that way and eventually I broke down and told my wife, Kristy, what was happening. By this time I was really starting to get paranoid. There was so much in the news about men getting breast cancer and I was greatly concerned. I did not have a doctor at the time; the one I had been seeing was no longer in private practice. Kristy called her doctor to get me an appointment . . . but they could not see me until October. She went ahead and made the appointment so I could get in with her doctor, but my lumpy nipple hurt, and I wasn't going to wait almost six months to get it checked out. That's when things began to get weird.

Kristy has a friend who is a gynecologist, and she called to ask his opinion about what I needed to do. He told her, "Tell Brian to come by the office tomorrow, and I'll check him out. Tell him to tell the receptionist that he is here to see me, and that I know what it's about." I know what you're thinking, because I was thinking the same thing: *How can this NOT go wrong?* It had disaster written all over it.

I showed up at his office the following day, and to say I was hesitant about stepping inside the doors would be an understatement akin to saying the *Titanic* had a slight mishap in the Atlantic Ocean. I was completely and utterly freaked out and my mind was not put at ease when I entered the waiting room. I looked around and there were at least half a dozen elderly ladies waiting patiently to be seen by the doctor. I walked up to the receptionist and said, "I'm Brian Gross. I'm here to see the doctor. He knows what it's about." She looked at me, clearly puzzled, but then said, "OK." I wondered how many other guys had come in and said the same thing. Thankfully, I didn't have to wait long before the good doctor came to get me because one can only stare at a floor for so long.

Unfortunately, being ushered back to the exam room did nothing to allay the hurricane of nerves I had swirling in my stomach. The doctor grabbed me by the elbow and almost started running down the hallway. I had the impression he really didn't want anyone to see him with me. The whole time he was muttering something incomprehensible to himself before saying, "Come on." When he finally got me into an exam room, he decided it was not the right place, and we then went in search of another room and found one: a storage room/broom closet. Actually, it had been an examination room at one time but was now the catch-all for things that weren't currently being used. Before rushing out of the room, he looked at me and said, "Take your shirt off." When he was in the hall, I overheard him tell a nurse, "There's a man in this room. Don't let anyone else go in there."

The wait seemed to last forever and it was pretty cold in the room. It struck me as a little strange that he had instructed no one to come into the room, but it also helped to calm my nerves for a few minutes as I stared at myself in the large mirror that was directly across from the chair in which I was sitting. There are many thoughts that rush through the mind of a nearly 400-pound, topless man as he sits in solitude, ogling himself in a large mirror. One of those thoughts was, *I'm glad he told the nurse to not let anyone come in here.*

Of course, someone didn't get the memo, and the look on the poor lady's face when she walked into the supply room and saw me sitting there bare-chested was beyond compare. I guarantee that a very large, half-naked man was the last thing she was expecting to see at work that day. She didn't know what to say and neither did I, so we just looked at each other for a few seconds, and then she mumbled something, grabbed what she was looking for and made a beeline for the door. I was wishing I could do the same thing. As she closed the door, I could hear her as she asked someone, "What is that man doing here?" The nurse who epically failed to keep anyone out replied, "He's here to see the doctor. No one was supposed to go in there."

From that point on I was taking no chances. I put my shirt back on while the storm in the pit of my stomach continued to rage. Shortly thereafter the doctor came back in and looked at me with an odd expression. He said, "I thought I told you to take your shirt off." Then he thought for a second and followed that up with, "Oh, yeah . . . the nurse. OK, just pull your shirt up." He felt around my right breast for a few minutes, found the nodule, and asked some cursory questions. Upon completing the examination, he said, "I'm pretty sure the lump isn't serious. Losing weight will probably take care of it." I couldn't keep myself from thinking, *I've dodged another bullet.* I was abruptly brought out of my reverie, however, when he went on to tell me, "But just to make sure I want to get that checked out at the imaging center. Let's go up to the front desk so we can get you an appointment for a mammogram."

My mind started racing, and I wasn't so sure I heard him correctly. He assured me it was only to confirm the lump was what he thought it was and not something significant. He paraded me up to the receptionist I had spoken to earlier, and he said loud enough for the people in the building across the street to hear, "Call imaging and get this man scheduled for a mammogram." OK, so his volume was not quite that loud, but he was no longer acting as if this were some kind of clandestine mission, perhaps because the cover had been blown by the unsuspecting nurse.

As I was leaving the office, relief washed over me. I was glad to be getting out of that bizarre situation, and I was hanging onto the fact that he was reasonably sure it was nothing serious. I was a little freaked out by needing to have a mammogram, but the whole situation was beginning to get funnier. Being the self-deprecating soul I am, I couldn't help but wonder to myself, *When a man has a mammogram, is the proper term for it a man-mogram?* The thought made me chuckle at the humiliation

I had just subjected myself to and made me wonder what would be in store for me when I actually had my man-mogram.

May 2, 2012, The Day of the Man-Mogram

Other than Kristy, I had told no one of my ordeal at the gynecologist. I had debated telling my brothers, Artie and Greg, about it because they would have gotten a good laugh out of the story, but ultimately the embarrassment of the situation led me to reconsider that idea. I was just hoping the man-mogram would not be as emasculating as the gyno visit had been. Thankfully, that wish was granted, but the visit to the Women's Center was not without discomfort.

The appointment was scheduled for the following week, which was good for if it had been any longer I may have talked myself out of going. I was hoping the waiting room of the Women's Center would not be as full as the one at the doctor's office, and, much to my surprise, it wasn't. I was the only one there. The receptionist checked me in and said it would be just a few minutes. I didn't have to wait long and only one person came in while I was waiting. But as soon as the door opened and the technician called me back, I knew I was in for an awkward situation. I knew the technician. Our kids had gone to the same daycare for years, and I was just hoping she wouldn't recognize me.

She did and the first thing she said to me was, "How's Brayden doing? Is he playing baseball this year?" So much for her not recognizing me. I knew it was going to be weird to disrobe for whoever the technician was, but was it too much to ask for it to be someone I didn't know? I didn't think so, but here I found myself half-naked again, getting a breast exam from someone who knew my kids and wanted to engage in small talk. But the discomfort wasn't just emotional. The physical aspect of a man-mogram was pretty awkward as well.

For those guys who have never had the man-mogram, let me tell you, it's not fun. Imagine sticking your breast in a vise and getting it smashed. It wasn't painful but it was uncomfortable. In the end, however, it was worth all the embarrassment and emasculation that came with the entire experience to find out I had a relatively minor condition known as gynecomastia, or in layman's terms, an abnormal enlargement of the male breast.

I was greatly relieved to find out I didn't have cancer or any other serious disease. I had a condition that was sometimes painful but could be reversed if I lost weight. I had gotten a free pass once again, or so I thought at the time. Other than some humiliation and a sensitive nipple, I was pretty much unscathed. Kristy was quick to point out that I had a mammogram before she did, and not just any woman can make that claim about her husband. I tried to explain to her that she didn't understand the awkward predicament I had been in at the gynecologist's office and at the Women's Center. She rolled her eyes and began talking about twenty-seven months of prenatal care, three labors and deliveries, and annual visits to the gynecologist. I'm not sure what her point was, but I'm pretty sure she didn't get mine, and she certainly didn't sympathize with me.

Looking back, though, gynecomastia was the first sign of a more serious, underlying health problem. My blasé attitude toward the diagnosis and the doctor's assertion that I needed to lose weight had no impact on me. I shrugged it off and chose to act as if nothing had ever happened. As I stated earlier, Randy Travis knew what he was singing about. Hindsight is indeed 20/20 but when you see the truth for what you want it to be instead of what it actually is, you might as well be blind. After six months of doing nothing to improve my situation, it was time for the blinders to come off. This time, though, there was much more urgency.

Chapter 2

Infield Flies, EKGs, and Diarrhea

"Come to me, all of you who are tired and have heavy loads, and I will give you rest. Accept my teachings and learn from me, because I am gentle and humble in spirit, and you will find rest for your lives. The burden that I ask you to accept is easy; the load I give you to carry is light."

Matthew 11:28-30, *New Century Version*

"The most glorious moments in your life are not the so-called days of success, but rather those days when out of dejection and despair you feel rise in you a challenge to life, and the promise of future accomplishments."
Gustave Flaubert

I find it alarming how often we as humans take things for granted. We don't like to think we do, but we are only human and one of the things humans do is take things for granted. I freely admit I am guilty of doing so. And, as is so often the case, I was rudely presented a reality where I could no longer take certain things for granted.

When I went to bed on October 5, 2012, my biggest (and by far most petty) concern in life was the infield fly rule in Major League Baseball. You see, I am an Atlanta Braves super-fan, and the Braves happened to be playing the St. Louis Cardinals that evening in the first Wild Card Game in baseball history. Now, I was not a big fan of this newfangled system where a second wild card team was added in each league and the two teams would play in a one-game playoff to advance to the divisional series. The way this game turned out did nothing to endear me to the new format.

Let me set the stage for you (and if you aren't familiar with baseball, just bear with me for a minute): it was the bottom of the 8th, St. Louis leading 6-3, one out, runners on first and second when Atlanta rookie shortstop Andrelton Simmons hits a lazy fly ball to left field. St. Louis shortstop Pete Kozma drifts back into the outfield, peels off, and the ball falls harmlessly in between him and left fielder Matt Holliday. Bases loaded, one out and Braves slugger Brian McCann is coming to the plate. Alas, the baseball gods were not smiling on Atlanta. Inexplicably, left field umpire Sam Holbrook invoked the infield fly rule. The hitter was out, the runners advanced at their own risk, and chaos ensued. I couldn't believe what I had just witnessed.

My blood pressure was up, my nostrils were flared, I chucked something across the room, and nearly broke my hand when I smacked the floor. I have watched baseball my entire life and had never seen that type of call made in a game; and I conservatively estimate the number of games I have watched to be in the thousands. I'm a rational guy (most of the time), and I understand the intent of the infield fly rule is to keep the defense from duping the runners by letting the ball fall so they can turn an easy double or triple play. But the ball landed more than 200 feet from home plate! And what is the outfield ump doing calling an infield fly? Does that seem odd to anyone else?

Anyway, the Braves lost and I was steamed to the point I couldn't enjoy talking to my dad on his birthday, and my wife and kids were afraid to speak to me because I was in rabid fan mode. I hadn't been this crazed because of a baseball game since the 1999 World Series when the Braves laid a colossal egg against the Yankees, and I realized getting that bent out of shape over a game wasn't good for my health.

As a result of that terrible call, I wasn't able to sleep much that night and I hardly watched any of the subsequent games of the playoffs. But my ire over the infield fly rule and its application in the Wild Card Game quickly subsided as more pertinent issues arose. It was funny how something so trivial in my life became a burning issue and in a few short days was returned to its inconsequential place by a hard dose of reality. There is nothing like a bad doctor's visit to put things in proper perspective.

October 10

I don't know that I have ever met anyone who enjoys going to the doctor. Always in the past, going to the doctor meant getting some bad news and a lecture about being severely overweight. (Just so you know, I hate the terms obese and morbidly obese. I have no qualms about saying I was overweight or fat. Both sound much better to me than anything to do with obese.) I expected my cholesterol to be high, thought maybe my blood pressure would not be too good, and knew I would get a stern talking to about diet and exercise. Been there and done that before. Only it didn't happen that way.

This was the first time I had been to this doctor as my previous physician had decided to pursue another career in the medical field. I was a little nervous about seeing the new doc for a couple of reasons. One, she is my wife's doctor and that creates a familiarity that is good but also gives her way too much personal information about us. At least that was my reasoning. Second, did you get that I used the word she instead of he? I had never been to a female doctor before. (Scratch that. I had been to a female doctor, just not a doctor who happened to be female. You have to love a good play on words.) Something about going to a woman doctor was very intimidating for me, but I knew I needed to see a doctor and being intimidated by a girl was just something I would have to overcome.

The bad news started as soon as I stepped on the scale and saw some ugly numbers pop up in front of me. I knew I had gained back all the weight I had lost four years earlier but this couldn't be right, could it? The scale was actually showing that I weighed even more than I did in March 2008. It registered 377 pounds. I was not ready for that, even though I thought I would be. I was in trouble but I was holding out hope the scale would be the worst of the news. Wrong again.

After talking to Dr. Connett for a few minutes, she wanted to listen to my heart. I hopped onto the table and figured everything would be fine. My heart was one thing I had never had to worry about before so I boldly assumed that would be the case this time as well, until she said, "I'm getting an irregular beat. We need to do an EKG to check that out." I was starting to get nervous, and not just because I was going to have to disrobe to the waist and let a nurse put sticky pads all over my torso. I was supposed to be very still and breathe normally during the test, but I thought that was a lot to ask of someone who may now have a defective heart.

Waiting for the results of the EKG was miserable. I was trying to internalize that I may have a bad heart and it seemed as if the results were taking much longer than necessary. I also tried to convince myself that my heart was indeed healthy and the EKG would prove it, but my well-established pattern for being wrong that day was still holding true.

The doctor came back in and, devastation in her voice, said, "You failed your EKG. The readings even suggest that you've had a prior heart attack." I couldn't believe what I was hearing. This was the strangest thing I had ever had someone tell me. How could I have had a heart attack? Certainly you would know if something like that had happened to you, right? How could you not know? "We need to schedule you for a stress test first thing in the morning. We can't wait on this. You have to clear anything you have on your schedule for tomorrow morning; no matter what. You also need to come in Friday morning to get blood drawn. We need to find out what else is going on with you as quickly as possible."

I was shell-shocked. I wasn't able to respond to anything she had told me. I set up an appointment for the following week to get the results of my blood work and left. I don't remember driving home, but I remember going straight to my bedroom and lying down on the bed. I didn't turn on the lights. The numbness that had initially overtaken me was now gone. It had been replaced with mental anguish. Though my body still felt fine, my mind was crushed. How was I going to tell Kristy what was going on with me? This was so unfair to her. She had already been through so much in life and now I was going to let her down. How could I look my kids in the eyes that night and let them know everything was going to be OK with Daddy?

It wasn't much longer before Kristy arrived with the kids. She came to the bedroom to check on me and knew immediately something was not right. Spencer, my youngest son who was three at the time, came behind her and jumped on the bed and fell on top of me. I rolled over and covered my face and began to bawl quietly. I was overwhelmed. Kristy ushered the kids out of the room and held me for a few minutes until I could tell her what was going on. I was scared. This should not have been happening but it was. I told her what the doctor had said. As always, she was the Rock of Gibraltar. She said with confidence (a confidence I was not sure she actually had but she was able to make it convincing), "We'll get through this. Everything will be fine."

After several minutes, she went to fix dinner for the kids and left me alone with my thoughts. I was in a better place at that point than I had been earlier and was doing some soul-searching. I was a broken man in need of some help, and I knew where to look for it. Praying was nothing new for me; I had done it most of my life. The problem, though, was I had not been doing it with the regularity I needed to. I had been struggling with some matters of faith, and, as is often the case in those times, I turned further away from God instead of going to Him as I should. But in my hour of need, I was overcome with the need to pray and pour out the contents of my broken (maybe in more ways than one) heart. I prayed that evening like I hadn't prayed in years and by the time I was finished, I was at peace. Something changed in me that night; something that was going to have a positive influence on my life going forward. I knew things wouldn't be easy, but I knew what I had to do and there was no choice in the matter. From that point, I was going to start taking care of myself by living a healthy life, not just physically but spiritually as well, for my benefit and for the benefit of my family.

October 11

I was thirty-four years old and was by far the youngest person in the waiting room by at least fifteen years. Looking around, it was hard to comprehend. I even had one lady ask me, "How old are you, honey?" I answered politely and she replied, "Well, I certainly hope everything turns out OK for you." The fact was not lost on anyone in that room, though, that I was too young to be having tests done on my heart.

Generally speaking, I've always been a patient man, but waiting for my name to be called to do my stress test was trying that virtue. Actually, the phrase *stress test* is another funny play on words. I was preparing to test how much stress my heart could take but in waiting to do so the level of stress was testing my patience. Thankfully, it was little thoughts such as this that were able to keep me from driving myself completely insane.

Once I was taken back and hooked up to the monitors, I began to get uneasy. I had no idea what the results were going to show. They wouldn't let Kristy come back with me; in the event the test triggered a heart attack, they didn't need a hysterical spouse to deal with while trying to save my life. I completely understood the line of thinking, but it didn't make me feel any more at ease. I stared at the monitors and watched closely as my heart rate fluctuated a little but mostly stayed in the 90-beat-per-minute range. I was not sure where it was supposed to be, but the technician explained to me that they were going to try and get it up to the 160-170 range.

When the physician entered the room, my heart rate jumped more than 30 beats per minute and the doctor joked, "Looks like another case of 'white coat syndrome'." I didn't mind because I knew that meant less work I would have to do on the treadmill and the quicker I could leave. As it turned out, I was only on the treadmill for a little less than five minutes and was free to return home. I was glad to be leaving the hospital, but I knew waiting on the results would be even harder than the actual test had been.

At home, Kristy fixed me a turkey sandwich with a few chips. It was the first thing I'd eaten since lunch the previous day. Upon seeing the food, my stomach started to turn. The thought of eating anything was pretty scary. I knew I had let food consume me instead of me consuming it for nourishment. It had become my vice, my stress reliever, my comforter. I let it control me instead of me controlling it. I managed to get the sandwich in my stomach and Kristy made sure I was fine before going to work. I was left alone with my thoughts, and I can assure you that is not always the best place for me.

Looking for a distraction, I picked up the phone and called my mom. I needed to tell her what was going on. I'm a very private person but I had to let the people who care about me know what was going on. It wouldn't be fair to them if something serious was going on with me and I let them get blindsided by tragic news. Besides, I needed to hear Mom's voice, and ask her and Dad to say some prayers for me.

Before I go any further, I want to tell you a little bit about my parents. My mom is an exceptional woman. I know I can tell her anything and she will be understanding and compassionate. She had been through some things most never experience. Just months after having my sister, Tonya, my dad was drafted into the military during the Vietnam War. He spent most of the next two years serving his country while she was left at home with a newborn. While Dad was overseas in Korea, she was the one raising a child without knowing if she would ever see her husband again. Several years later, her mother, grandfather, and uncle were all killed in an automobile accident. Her grandfather was more like her father and she actually called him "Dad" most of the time. I can't imagine losing one person so close to me in a tragic accident, let alone three. My mom is tough as nails, but she's also as nurturing as any one person can be.

My dad is the wisest person I've ever met and I often go to him looking for sage advice. I'm not sure if he realizes how profound he is, but he almost always leaves me with something to think about. As hard as it was for Mom when Dad was in the military, just imagine how hard it was for him being away from his wife and newborn child. He missed several major milestones that could never be replaced, but he was answering the call of his country and was proud to serve. He set the example for my brothers and me for what it means to be a father. I've always said if I could be half the father he is, then I have more than done my job as a parent. I can always go to Dad when I have a question regarding faith and he always has an answer.

When it comes to parents, I have been truly blessed. I can't imagine anyone having a better set of parents than my siblings and I. They've set an example I hope I can replicate and set for my children. There were times when I had let them down and disappointed them, but they had never turned their backs on me or made me feel like less of a person for my mistakes. Their love is unconditional; no strings attached. I knew when I made this call it would be as hard for them to hear as it was for me to say, but I owed it to them. With much trepidation, I picked up the phone and placed the call.

Mom knew something was up when I called because normally I would have been at work shortly after noon on a Thursday. Usually when I called like that she knew one of the kids was sick. But not this time. After exchanging a few pleasantries, I managed to say, "I guess you're wondering why I called. I had a stress test today." I told her what was going on with me and she listened, which is one of her greatest qualities.

"Remember, your dad failed an EKG a few years ago. He passed his stress test with no problems." She remained calm the whole time, her voice unwavering and strong. She knew exactly what I needed to hear. She concluded the phone call by saying, "Keep us updated and take care of yourself. I love you." Even though it was not a phone call I wanted to make, it made me feel better. After all, I didn't actually feel bad, and I was convinced there was nothing wrong with my heart, so maybe everything would be just fine.

The comfort lasted throughout the day, but quickly vanished when it was time to go to bed. I lay in the bed for several minutes just staring at the dark ceiling, listening to myself breathe. I hated to admit it but I was afraid to go to sleep. What if the EKG was right? What if my ticker was bad? I didn't want to have a heart attack in my sleep! What if I couldn't get Kristy awake to get help in time? See what I mean about being alone with my thoughts?

When I finally drifted off to sleep, it was a matter of minutes before I bolted upright in bed. This happened a few more times before I woke Kristy up and told her I was too afraid to sleep. She comforted me and I finally drifted off to sleep more peacefully. All in all, I probably woke up at least ten times that night.

The next morning I reported back to the doctor's office to have blood drawn so they could run a battery of tests to see what else was going on with me. I always dread having blood drawn because I'm not an easy stick. My veins don't like to cooperate. The most consistent place for success in blood drawing is from my hand and I have discovered over the years that there are many nurses who don't like drawing from the hand (some won't even try to draw from there). Personally, my thought is I would rather them try to get it from a place that tends to work, even if it is a little painful, than to have them dig around in my arms with a needle and have no luck and then draw it from my hand. It just makes sense to me.

Later that day the doctor's office called to tell me the results of the stress test. I wasn't expecting to hear from them until Monday. I was glad they called, however, because the stress test showed my heart was fine. A huge burden had been lifted. I had dodged a major bullet. Now I just needed to await the results of my blood work.

October 18

I anticipated my visit to the doctor wasn't going to be pleasant, but I had no idea it was going to be as bad as it turned out to be. A few days before my appointment, the doctor's office called me at work. "Mr. Gross? This is a nurse from Dr. Connett's office. Is there any way you can come to the office today? She would like to discuss some of the results of your blood work."

As you can imagine, I became a little panicked. "I can come right now," I managed to reply, but they couldn't get me in until four o'clock. "I can't make it then. I have to be at home when my son gets off the school bus. Can it just wait a couple days until my appointment?"

That's when things became uneasy. The nurse stuttered and stammered for a second before finally blurting out, "You're a new diabetic and you really need to come in and see the doctor." I was taken aback. I thought my ears were deceiving me. At first, I was shocked. But just as quickly, I knew it was no surprise. My mom is diabetic and with the weight I had been carrying on my body, I was definitely a high-risk case. Coming to this realization didn't make the words any easier to hear. Finally, with the doctor in her ear telling her what to say, the nurse said, "Don't eat any carbohydrates, breads, sugars, pastas, sweets, or anything like that until you see Dr. Connett."

I hung up the phone and stood in my empty classroom feeling as if I had been hit in the gut with a bowling ball. I had played with fire most of my life and had finally gotten burned. I knew I could not continue treating my body like trash and expect it to be a well-oiled machine. And the worst part about it: I had brought leftover pasta with me for my lunch. What a bummer! I snuck away from work during lunch, went to Chick-fil-A, and ate a grilled chicken sandwich, no bun, while alone in my van feeling sorry for myself.

While waiting for my appointment, I made a list of questions to ask the physician, and Kristy made arrangements to go along with me. I knew it wouldn't be an enjoyable experience, but I thought I'd be prepared this time. As it turned out, despite being right about my heart, I was wrong a whole lot more than I'd been right in the past week. The lone highlight of the whole visit came when I stepped on the scale and was already down to 363. I had lost fourteen pounds in eight days. I had shocked my system by losing my appetite and being mortified around food and it had worked—for a week.

When Dr. Connett came into the room, she got right down to business. The first thing she discussed was the diabetes. My blood glucose level was over 220. I knew from my mom's experience as a diabetic that normal range fell between 70-120. I also knew sugar levels could fluctuate greatly depending on a variety of factors so I wasn't overly concerned about that number. Then she started talking about something called an A1C. "The A1C is the way your body measures your sugar level over a period of time. It's supposed to be below 5.8; anything between 5.9 and 6.4 is considered pre-diabetic. You are at 7.9, which means you are a full-blown diabetic," she said. Since I was not familiar with this measurement, and based on the way she was presenting it to me, I was hearing that my blood was sweeter than a tablespoon of sugar dipped in honey and washed down with Mountain Dew. This was not good.

But then she kept going. Apparently I wasn't just diabetic. "Unfortunately, diabetes isn't your only problem. You have hypothyroidism and you'll need to take medication for that the rest of your life. You have high cholesterol, high triglycerides, low testosterone and a fatty liver. Your liver function is dangerously low." I wasn't surprised by the thyroid, cholesterol, and triglycerides but the last two really got to me. The low testosterone shouldn't have been all that surprising, considering my visit in May to the gynecologist, but it was still emasculating to hear. (I know, I know. The man-mogram was emasculating enough.) The fatty liver, though, was frightening. I wasn't sure how bad it really was but I knew the liver was a vital organ and covering it in layers of fat until it practically quits functioning wasn't good for one's longevity. The good doc was so concerned that she wanted to do a liver ultrasound to rule out other problems and she wanted me to do more blood work to check some liver levels.

At this point, I shut down. I had my list of questions, and I couldn't bring myself to ask them. Kristy asked a few but I had zoned out. I was staring at the floor, not wanting to make eye contact with Dr. Connett. The way she spoke to me and the way she looked at me made me sick because all I could see and hear was pity. I hate when people feel sorry for me or pity me. I know now she is passionate about her patients and she was just deeply concerned about my well-being, but at the time all I could feel was pity and it made me mad. I'm sure I was just trying to deflect what she was telling me, and I was projecting blame on her instead of accepting my role in creating this monster, but I could not look at her. This was why I was apprehensive about a woman doctor. I would much rather be chewed out or given a rah-rah speech instead of being pitied. I wanted to leave or crawl into a hole or just teleport myself out of there like Harry Potter. If only I had some floo powder.

It wasn't time to leave, though. I had yet to hear her recommended treatment. She told me to drop a hundred pounds (she never made mention of the fourteen I had already lost) and see what that did for my testosterone, liver function, and cholesterol. The only medication she was putting me on was a pill for my underactive thyroid and a pill to regulate my insulin production called Metformin, which came with a verbal warning. She told me, "This pill will upset your stomach. You will have diarrhea. There are going to be times over the next two weeks when you hate my guts for putting you on this but you have to take it." At first I thought it would be no big deal, but given my track record the past week, I thought better of taking it lightly, and I am glad I didn't begin taking the medication with a cavalier attitude.

Needless to say I was depressed the rest of the evening. I was upset with myself. I wasn't sure how I had let myself get in such poor physical shape. By all accounts, I was a young man who should have a long, happy life ahead of me. I was mad and I wanted to be mad at Dr. Connett, but I knew where to place the blame. I did some more intense soul-searching and laid it out in prayer. I truly was able to let go and let God. I had made major changes in the past week, and I was determined to make sure these changes were permanent, but I was going to need all the help I could get in the days ahead.

The following week was like none I had ever experienced. I began taking the Metformin, and everything she had told me about it was accurate. The first time I took the medication was on a Friday night. We ate a nice family dinner and followed it up by decorating foam pumpkins to put up on the kitchen cabinets for Halloween. Less than an hour after taking the evil pill, I had to make a mad dash for the bathroom. My stomach was under attack and I had no time to spare.

Kristy's parents came for a weekend visit the following day, and I wasn't ready to tell them about my ailments just yet, so I spent the better part of Saturday sneaking off to use the bathroom as discreetly as possible. The next day, though, I could no longer hide how I was feeling. We went to eat lunch after church at Outback Steakhouse. I made it through the meal just fine, but then I broke out in a cold sweat and my stomach began turning somersaults and cramping. I had to excuse myself and go sit in the van with the air conditioner running. I was miserable and, at that moment, I did indeed hate the good doctor. I wasn't sure I could get through the next couple of weeks. The one thought that kept racing through my mind was, *Why do I feel so much worse now than I did before?*

Chapter 3

The Times Are a Changin'

"Jesus Christ is the same yesterday, today, and forever."
Hebrews 13:8, *New Century Version*

*"Progress is impossible without change, and those who
cannot change their minds cannot change anything."*
George Bernard Shaw

My life was changing at a breakneck pace and I was OK with that. I mean, really I didn't have a choice but to be good with it because it was necessary. For years I had abused my body and now I was paying the piper. I had neglected my own health for too long and it was finally catching up to me. I had lost seventy-five pounds from March 2008 through the end of that year and was able to keep it off until the middle of 2009. We had just had our second child, Laura-Rae, in January 2008, and Kristy and I were both ready for a transformation. We were the parents of two now and wanted to set a good example for our kids. We joined Weight Watchers once she was healed from her C-section and could start exercising without pain. For the first time ever, I had found a weight-loss program that worked for me.

The results were rapid and impressive. I wasn't doing much as far as exercise, but changing the way I ate and having Kristy as my partner on this mission were all I really needed. We began cooking at home much more, something we have always enjoyed doing but we had let fall by the wayside, and we were using several recipes from the Weight Watchers website. Cooking and eating healthy was actually becoming fun. I saw my weight plummet from 370 to 295. I was feeling good about myself. Kristy dropped nearly sixty pounds and we were both happier about ourselves and our health than we had been in a long time.

But as is constant in life, changes were coming. In January 2009, a few days after Laura-Rae's first birthday, we found out we were expecting another child. The problem was we weren't really sure when the baby was due because this was definitely an unexpected pregnancy. Kristy had begun taking a low dosage of her birth control pills and was still nursing Laura-Rae. It wasn't supposed to happen.

We did some quick calculating and estimated the new baby could arrive anywhere from late July to the end of September. The timing of the pregnancy wasn't the least bit ideal for us. We had adjusted to having a second child, we had developed a healthy lifestyle, and Kristy was finally ready to take a break from nursing. She wasn't mentally ready to go through another pregnancy on the heels of the last one. From the time she became pregnant with Laura-Rae in April 2007 until the time she quit nursing Spencer in May 2010, she spent thirty-seven consecutive months where she was either pregnant, breastfeeding, or both. It didn't take a genius to figure out she was overwhelmed and susceptible to falling back into old habits. I was able to resist for a short period of time but eventually I caved in and all the hard work I put in for more than a year was all for naught.

When the doctor first told me what was going on, I knew in my heart that this time would be different because it had to be. Even when I had lost seventy-five pounds, I was never convinced I was going to keep it off. It sounded good to talk like I would and that I had made a complete lifestyle change, but I never believed it deep down inside my soul. I had tried to do it my way before and it had worked for a time but eventually I gave up. Not this time. The Lord had convicted me and I knew I was guilty. I was going to do my best to do it His way this time and not interfere with Him. I had no desire to have my wife and kids watch me as I tortured and destroyed my body. It wasn't too late to alter my ways, if I could only stay off the toilet long enough to do something about it.

October 27-28

Both my parents and Kristy's live in Jackson, Ky., where both of us were raised. We live in Russell, Ky., now, a small town not much larger than Jackson and more than 100 miles away, so we don't always get to see our family as much as we would like. When possible, we try to get back "home" at least once a month and usually more than that around the holidays. The last weekend of October was going to be our first visit to Jackson since my diagnoses. We were leaving Saturday morning and hoping to get there in time for kickoff of the Kentucky/Missouri football game. (I'm an avid UK football fan. That makes me an oddity in this basketball-crazed state, but I can't help it.)

I was still feeling miserable most of the time but accepted that it was going to be another week or so before I started turning the corner, based on what Dr. Connett had told me. I was eating better, and I had hoped to be burning up the treadmill each day when I came home from work, but the constant diarrhea and the intense stomach cramps were making that impossible. I was getting frustrated, but was trying to remain positive. It would be easy to give in, but I was determined to not do that. I had given in too many times, and I was trying to put those days behind me.

I had my liver ultrasound a few days before we went to Jackson, and I wasn't too concerned about the results. As with my heart, I was pretty sure my liver was fine. Maybe it was just wishful thinking, but I was convinced the ultrasound would show nothing, and I was right. The worst part about the process was the technician pressing the wand into my ribs. That probably doesn't sound too bad to most of you, but it was torture to me. You see, I have this weird idiosyncrasy about things touching or putting pressure on my bones. Kristy thinks it's ridiculous, but it makes sense to me to not have things touching your bones. It just feels awkward. Sometimes when she is goofing around with me, Kristy will grab my wrist and squeeze or begin poking me in the collarbone. It's excruciating! I think the Department of Defense or Homeland Security could learn a few things from her technique.

Other than the liver not having any major issues, the best news of that day came when I stepped onto the scale. I was down to 354. In just fifteen days I had been able to lose twenty-three pounds. I was amazed. I had completely transformed my eating habits and my body was responding. My only concern was that I had completely cut out all carbs from my diet. I knew I couldn't keep doing that; my body did need some carbs to function. But I was afraid to eat them. The doc said to lay off carbohydrates, so I was laying off.

I also picked up my meter for checking my blood sugar. I wasn't really sure how to use it, though. The nurse just gave it to me and, without showing me anything, said, "Check your sugar levels three or four times a week and make sure you check it first thing in the morning and two hours after meals." The thought of jabbing a sharp object into the tip of my finger made me very apprehensive. What made it worse was that I had no idea how to put the guard on the lancet so the first time I checked my sugar, I stabbed my middle finger with an exposed lancet. It took three test strips before getting a reading on the meter and it showed my blood glucose level was 51. There was no way that could be right, was there? Just two weeks ago it was running in the 220s. I assumed the thing wasn't accurate, so I decided not to use it anymore until I visited the diabetes consultant at the hospital the following week.

Now I just had to face the obstacle of visiting the family in Jackson. We were staying at my parents' house, which presented me with a large hurdle to jump. My mom is an amazing cook. It's very difficult to not eat heaping amounts of food when she fixes something. Even though she has only been cooking for herself and Dad the past several years, it is nothing for her to fix enough food at a time to feed an army (which is necessary when all my family is gathered around). Being the understanding woman she is and knowing my plight, she fixed a nice lunch of chicken salad and fruit. It was great, but my raging stomach issues took exception to it, as with everything else I had eaten over the past week.

The real problem came the next day when I drank a cup of coffee. The straight shot of caffeine mixed with the sugary creamer wasn't good for me. My body hadn't had caffeine or sugar for nearly two and a half weeks and it wasn't happy about it. I began to feel jittery and nervous. I broke out into a cold sweat and was beginning to get worried. A few hours later my sugar level bottomed out. I was more miserable than I had been in a long time, and it was starting to wear on me. I wasn't expecting getting healthy to be this physically taxing. I was afraid to eat, I was afraid not to eat. I was confused and frustrated. I was to meet with the diabetic specialist for a consultation in two more days, and I was hoping she would have some good advice for me. Above all, I think I really wanted her to tell me the worst of it was nearly over.

October 30

I was a little nervous about going to the diabetes specialist, but I was not dreading meeting her. I was holding out hope she would provide me with some comfort and knowledge. Kristy once again made arrangements to go with me. It was important for her to hear what the consultant had to say so she could help me with whatever I needed to do. I had my list of questions, and I was determined to not freeze up this time. I already knew what was going on with me so there was no reason to feel sorry for myself anymore. I needed useful information, and that's just what the consultant provided.

The first thing the consultant did was make us feel welcome and put our minds at ease. She had the records from my doctor's visit so she was familiar with what was going on without me having to rehash everything. She opened up about herself and her experiences being a diabetic. She went over my numbers, the blood glucose level and the A1C, and explained to me that my numbers were not nearly as bad as some she had seen. That made me feel better because it told me that my condition might be much easier to control than I originally thought.

Then the conversation shifted to eating. "What have you been eating since being diagnosed as a diabetic?" she asked. "Walk me through each meal."

"I eat a banana or apple with a cup of coffee sweetened with sugar-free creamer for breakfast. A turkey sandwich with cheese on wheat bread for lunch and baked chicken and roasted vegetables for dinner."

"Do you have any snacks throughout the day?"

"I usually eat a fiber brownie. That's about it," I answered.

"That's not enough. You need to make sure you're getting between 45 and 60 grams of carbohydrates a meal and between 135 and 180 grams per day. You can't be afraid to eat carbs. You need them. The key is to make sure you eat something high in protein when you eat carbs. You need to eat three regular meals a day and have two snacks a day. Do you carry any candy with you?"

I wasn't expecting her to ask me that. "No," I answered, thinking the answer should have been obvious.

"You need to make sure you keep a bag of candy with you just in case your sugar levels drop. Make sure you have something that is almost purely sugar. You don't need anything chocolate or that has fat in it. The body will use the fat before it uses the carbs. Now, you need to understand that I'm not giving you license to scarf down Sweet Tarts whenever you want to."

I was a little surprised at what she was telling me. The news was getting better. Then, she gave me the most encouraging piece of advice yet. "It really is fine to eat some things that aren't very good for you sometimes. If you really want it, eat it. Depriving yourself of something you love will only decrease your odds of being successful in managing your diabetes."

That wasn't even the highlight of the visit, though. "Let me see you poke your finger," she said. I recounted my misadventure from a few days earlier and told her, "I think I was doing it wrong." She agreed with my assessment.

"Your first mistake was not having the guard on the lancet correctly and exposing the needle point. Never poke yourself with an exposed lancet." She put the cap on the device for me, and then I poked my finger only to have no blood come from my fingertip. I set the dial higher on the lancet so it would strike my fingertip with more force. Again, there was no blood.

"I don't understand what I'm doing wrong. Why doesn't this thing work?" I grumbled. Before I could say anything else, she grabbed my hand, lowered it between my knees, squeezed my finger, and a bubble of blood appeared. Then she grabbed my meter and placed the strip near the edge of the blood bubble. The meter registered 91. She was surprised my level was that low, but that reading told her how much I had actually been avoiding carbs.

"Two hours after eating, your glucose level should be below 180. For what we call a fasting measure, like when you poke your finger first thing in the morning, it should be below 140." She gave me a few more pointers about finger-poking, and I realized it was not going to be as difficult as I had anticipated.

Before leaving, she gave me a three-month plan which included walking or exercising for thirty minutes, checking my feet, and eating three meals and two snacks each day. I assured her I would follow her orders, and she assured me I was nearing the end of the road with my stomach issues. For the first time in three weeks, I felt like my whole world was not crashing down around me. I had gotten off to a great start and was making tremendous progress. I was now equipped with the knowledge I would need to follow through on my new lifestyle. I was becoming more comfortable with what life was going to be like. I just had to clear one last hurdle and I would be on my way.

November 12

Kristy and I had made plans to go to Barboursville, W.Va., to do some Christmas shopping for the kids. I had taken a personal day and she didn't have to go to her office that day because it was Veteran's Day. She always tells people one of the perks of being a banker is that you get off for all federal holidays. I always thought that as a teacher I should get those days off too but it doesn't always work that way.

The day before, we had taken our oldest child, Brayden, to his first NFL game. He has been a huge New York Giants football fan since he was two. The opening weekend of the 2007 NFL season we happened to be watching the Giants play the Dallas Cowboys. Brayden became enamored with the team in blue and their quarterback Eli Manning. The Giants went on to lose that game and then we watched them again the following week and they lost once more, this time to the Green Bay Packers. I told Brayden he may want to check into getting a new team. He was undeterred and continued to get excited any time the Giants were on television. As it turned out, his devotion to the 0-2 Giants paid off. The G-men went on a tear in December and throughout the playoffs, leading to a clash against the undefeated, 18-0 New England Patriots. In a stunning thriller, the Giants were able to upset the Pats in Super Bowl XLII.

But the 2012 Giants were much different from the 2007 version we were watching play in Cincinnati against the Bengals. I was really hoping the Manning-led Giants would play well with Brayden in attendance. They had struggled their previous two games, but the Bengals has been scuffling more. What better way to break out of a slump than to play a team on a long losing streak? Well, the slump was broken; the Bengals' slump that is. Right from the opening kickoff, Cincinnati dominated the game. I kept holding out hope, but after consecutive Giants' drives in the third quarter ended with Eli interceptions, I knew it was all over but the crying. The final score was 31-13, and it wasn't even that close. I was proud of Brayden for holding it together. He was upset and near tears a few times but was able to keep his composure. After the game, he told me, "I've never had a least favorite football team until today. Now, I do. The Bengals." The irony in that is Spencer now proclaims himself a Bengals fan. I have no idea where he got that from, but it certainly wasn't me.

While we were in Cincinnati and Northern Kentucky, I ate a little less healthy but I was not out of control. But you can only eat so much greasy, yet very good, pizza and not pay a price for it. On the way home that night, we had to make an emergency pit stop just outside of Maysville at a gas station. Anyone who knows me well knows that I hate having to use public facilities, but my choices this time were limited. I could either make a mess in my pants, which I'm sure Kristy and the kids would not have appreciated in the confines of a minivan, or I could suck it up and go to the gas station. I was hoping that it was a one-time thing, but I was pretty sure it wouldn't be.

Now, in Barboursville, my finicky stomach continued to plague me. Before finishing my meal at Chili's, I had to excuse myself to the restroom. As soon as we got to the mall, I had to sprint to the restroom in Dick's Sporting Goods. And before we could go to a parent/teacher meeting at school with Brayden's teacher, we had to stop at our house so I could answer nature's call. I was unable to enjoy most of the day because I felt as if I had been run over by a semi. Not only was my stomach a concern, I had broken out into a cold sweat that just would not go away. Just when I thought I had turned the corner, I had my most miserable day in a few weeks. I was rapidly becoming a public bathroom connoisseur; the thought of which did nothing to help my ailing stomach.

The good news, though, was this day was truly the last miserable day that I had. From that point forward, my stomach issues were controlled and life was returning to normal. I was able to finally get on the treadmill and do some walking; something I hadn't been able to do while my stomach was tormenting me. I'd found my groove and was looking forward to the approaching holiday season. I was anxious about Thanksgiving because that's the one day that is set aside for the purpose of being a glutton. (OK, just so you know, I know it's about giving thanks to God for all of His blessings, but we do that by stuffing ourselves to the gills, right?) I knew if I could survive the next two weeks, everything would be OK.

Chapter 4

Peace in the Valley

"I have told you all this so that you may have peace in me. Here on earth you will have many trials and sorrows. But take heart, I have overcome the world."
John 16:33, *New Living Translation*

"Above all the grace and the gifts that Christ gives to His beloved is that of overcoming self."
St. Francis of Assisi

Just a couple of months before being diagnosed with diabetes, I self-published a couple of stories through Amazon. They were both Christmas stories and were parts one and two of a series. I'd written both stories several years earlier and had never done anything with them. Since they were both too short to be a conventional book they would be a tough sell to any publisher. But in today's media-savvy world, there is a place for everything. I published the stories in mid-August with hopes of them being bestsellers by the time Santa Claus came to town.

In an effort to boost my profile as a writer, and to hopefully draw more attention to my work, I began writing a blog. I titled my blog *Through My Four Eyes* and its primary focus was Major League Baseball and NCAA Football, with most of the attention being directed to the Atlanta Braves and the University of Kentucky. I was pretty sure I would be the only blogger out there with that specific focus so the question became: how do you get people to read what you write?

For the first six weeks of writing, I was on fire. I was cranking out about three blogs per week. I was getting some feedback, mostly from people I knew really well, but it was encouraging. I was excited about what I was doing. I hadn't written anything earth-shattering, but my blogs were causing some debates when I was around family, friends, or co-workers, and that was an exhilarating feeling.

I was hoping to write something that would get noticed, and I believed if I kept doing what I was doing, it would only be a matter of time. Within the first month of writing, my blog had more than 1,000 page views. I had written on a variety of subjects within the two fields I had assigned myself. One of the most debated was a piece I wrote after Neil Armstrong passed away. Being a history teacher who loves reading about the advent of the American space program, I could not pass up the opportunity to compile a team of MLB players who were born after Mr. Armstrong made his historic "giant leap for mankind." The debate over who was not on that list and why one player was picked over another was fascinating.

My favorite piece, however, was a derisive, sarcastic missive directed at my least favorite team in all of sports, the Notre Dame Fighting Irish. I called them out on several different aspects of what they have become and for having a self-inflated opinion of their place in today's college football world. Well, thankfully, not many people actually read that blog because I ended up with some egg on my face after their miraculous run to the BCS National Championship game against Alabama. I don't retract what I said in the blog, but the Irish did have a season that put them back on the college football map much to my chagrin.

Writing my blog was a great outlet for me. I was having more fun researching ideas, writing, comparing statistics, predicting games, and posting finished pieces than I'd had in a long time. I was making a list of possible topics for the upcoming weeks, circling games on the NCAA schedule to preview, and checking baseball stats constantly. I had a new hobby and it was phenomenal, but there was always a feeling I could be doing more with it. I wasn't exactly sure what else I could do but there was a persistent, nagging feeling in the back of my mind.

From August 18 through October 4, I posted nineteen blogs on *Through My Four Eyes*. The ensuing weekend was the opening round of the MLB playoffs so I anticipated I would have plenty of fodder for the mill, but all that changed with an infield fly call on the night of October 5. I needed to give myself some time to cool down before writing anything. I had a mini-fall break from school that weekend, so I was just going to enjoy the break and spend the time with my family, watching as little baseball as possible. It sounded like a great plan to me.

But then life got in the way as it so often does. October 10 rolled around and my world was turned upside down. For obvious reasons, the concerns over my health moved my newfound hobby to the backseat. At first, I totally lost the desire to put words on paper. I was consumed with figuring out what was wrong with me and how I could fix it. People began to ask me when I was going to post another blog. I had no answer. Kristy kept encouraging me to write something. I couldn't. The fire was gone. I wasn't sure if it would ever come back. In forty-eight days, I had posted nearly twenty blogs. It would be another forty-nine days before the urge to write struck me again, and when it did, I had something different to say.

November 22

When November rolls around, I usually only have one thing on my mind and that is the upcoming holidays. To me, it just doesn't get any better than Thanksgiving and Christmas. I mean, the former is a celebration of being thankful in which we practice eating until we are in a petrified state, and the latter is a celebration of the birth of the Messiah, Jesus Christ. If you can't get excited about those two things, what can move you to get excited about anything?

Even with everything that was going on with me, I was still excited about Thanksgiving. It was going to be a great challenge, but I was feeling good about the way things were going. I was starting to get in a groove and gain some confidence. My last day at work before going on Thanksgiving break was Friday, November 16, and that was also my last chance for a weigh-in until after the break. (This is where I must make another embarrassing confession. My scale at home only registers up to 330 pounds, so I had to use the medical scale at work to get an official weigh-in.) When I stepped on the scale, I saw something fantastic. I was able to slide the scale down to 300 and go up from there. I checked in at 347 pounds and was absolutely thrilled. I had lost thirty pounds in a little more than five weeks. What an awesome way to start the Thanksgiving break!

A month before I was as low as I'd ever been, and now I was starting to see some light at the end of the tunnel. I was already starting to get back into some clothes that had been just taking up space in my closet. Just guessing, I could only wear approximately 20 percent of the clothes in my wardrobe before I started dropping some weight. I was on the verge of having to replace an entire closet full of useless clothing, a thought that was as much humbling as it would be expensive. But not now. Finally, I was able to start getting back into some clothes that hadn't been worn in a few years. And the best discovery was that I was finally able to comfortably get into a pair of jeans Kristy had gotten me for Christmas in 2011.

I was also feeling better. When asked by my doctor a month earlier if I had been feeling bad, I answered no, and I was being honest. I wasn't trying to hide or deny anything. I truly didn't think I was feeling bad. A month of eating better and taking medication for my diabetes and thyroid said otherwise. Looking back, I hadn't been feeling nearly as well as I had thought. I was no longer drained of energy when I would get home from school. I had gotten to the point that when I went home, I would sit down and fall asleep with no warning and could be out for half an hour or more. I couldn't make myself stay awake. I just assumed that maybe I wasn't getting enough quality sleep. In the middle of the night, I would wake up and have to use the bathroom because my bladder was aching. I figured it was because I was drinking too much water too close to bedtime. Neither of these things had ever been a problem before, but I thought it was just part of getting older. As I found out during my consultation with the diabetes specialist, these are common symptoms for many diabetics.

Those were not the only problems I was having, however. For about two months before going to the doctor, my left knee was constantly barking. I knew I was extremely overweight and wasn't doing my knees any favors. I self-diagnosed the problem as the onset of arthritis in that knee; no biggie as I had arthritis in other places as well. But once I started to shed some weight and eat better, the achy knee quit bothering me. I was moving around better than I had in months, maybe even years.

And then there was the swelling I had in my ankles and lower legs. I had chalked it up to extra weight, water retention, being on my feet at work, bad shoes, and an old pickup basketball injury to my right ankle in high school. The ankle had bothered me for twenty years, aching and swelling off and on, so it stood to reason that was still part of the problem. As you can probably tell, I was making a lot of excuses for myself, and rather poor ones at that. I was turning a blind eye to what was happening to me. It was amazing how when I started to address my health issues, the swelling went down and Kristy even made the comment, "Hey, you have ankles again." I had to admit it felt pretty good to look down, and see my lower legs looking normal and not looking like small tree stumps.

In a month's time, I had run the gamut of emotions. I was the lowest I had ever been, scared out of my mind that I was going to leave Kristy alone to raise our three kids. Then, I was relieved I didn't have a heart condition, which was followed by wallowing in self-pity because of the awful doctor's report. The pity party was replaced by misery over the adjustment to my meds and eventually excitement about the way things were finally going. It was one of the longest, most up-and-down months of my life and now the ups were much more common than the downs. What a rollercoaster!

After all I had been through, I was looking forward to Turkey Day, a day in which I've historically punished my body with reckless abandon. This year was really going to be a difference-maker for me. I had transformed my eating habits and felt as if I had control over what I was putting into my body instead of letting it have control over me. I was the captain of this ship, not the turkey, gravy, beans, rolls, butter, macaroni and cheese, and dressing before me. If I could clear this obstacle, I would be on my way.

When it came time to eat, I let everybody else go through the line before me. When all my family is gathered in one place, we could easily field a small football team. Just including my parents, my three siblings and their families, and my wife and kids, there are twenty-seven of us. Throw in various friends, boyfriends and girlfriends of my nieces and nephews, and other extended family, and the number easily sails into the mid-thirties. My strategy was to let most of them go first and maybe there wouldn't be much left to choose from. By the time I fixed my plate, everything was picked over, but there was still a good amount left. As I said earlier, my mom fixes enough food to feed an army.

I filled my Styrofoam compartment plate as full as I dared and noticed there was plenty of white space left. My goal for the dinner was to not stuff myself so I could eat a piece of pumpkin pie. I was comfortably full after eating and I didn't even go back for seconds. I waited about an hour before getting my piece of pie topped with whipped cream, and it was worth it. I hadn't had any kind of real sweets for a month and a half, and the pumpkin pie was heavenly. I checked my blood sugar a couple hours after eating the pie, and it was 98. I was amazed and definitely satisfied with the way the day had gone.

That night we were staying with Kristy's parents and after everybody went to bed, I reflected on how my life had changed in six weeks. I was amazed at the progress I had made. I was once again compelled to write. I had things I wanted to say, but this time I was changing focus. I was going to openly put my plight on paper and share it with whoever wanted to read it. Upon finishing my first blog in seven weeks, I was at peace. I fully accepted what was going on with me and what I was doing to correct it. But more importantly, it was time to give credit to the One who had lifted my burden and opened my eyes.

Changing Focus

As many of you have noticed, I have been on hiatus. Well, what better day to get back in the groove than Thanksgiving? Nothing gets me excited like stuffing myself to the gills and wallowing in misery the rest of the day. Of course, that was in years past. The days of gorging myself and living in gluttony have come to a screeching halt. As you will notice, the focus of my blog is going to shift slightly. I'm still going to comment on the goings-on in the world of sports, (I have missed so much in the last six weeks that has been worthy of discussion), but I will also be discussing recent developments in my life, and with the holidays upon us I will have some holiday-themed items as well.

As for the days of gorging myself and wallowing in my own gut-busting misery, there is a reason they have ended, and I wish it were just because I had finally decided to whip my tail into shape. The real reason for this lifestyle change is a negative doctor's report. Suffice it to say I have never felt so miserable in my life as I did when I left the doctor's office on the days of October 10 and 18. By the time it was all over, I had to deal with certain facts I was not ready to deal with. I have been diagnosed as a diabetic with high cholesterol and a messed-up thyroid. Not great news but better than the initial thought that I had heart problems according to an EKG I failed with flying colors. (Thankfully, after a stress test, we discovered the ticker was just fine.) My newly discovered ailments left me feeling out of sorts and struggling to grapple with my own mortality. I was glad I wasn't as bad off as originally thought, but I still had major issues to face and daunting obstacles ahead.

It was at this moment that I decided to turn things over to a higher power and pray for my health to improve, but more importantly to find the resolve to face the challenges that lay before me. I have been guilty in the past of not putting God first in my life and only turning to Him in times of desperate need. Well, this was a time of desperation and my daily life was going to have to undergo a major overhaul.

On this day of thanks, I am very thankful for my health and that I was able to discover these problems before they became too serious. I'm proud to say that in the forty-three days since I initially went to the doctor, I have now lost thirty pounds. I hope to be able to lose another twenty before going back to the doctor in January. I'm also pleased to say that after eating my paltry, yet satisfying, meal (complete with pumpkin pie), my blood sugar checked in at a cool 98, well within the parameters the diabetic specialist laid out for me. Today was a great success in my book.

This ordeal, while difficult, has been a great life lesson for me. I've played with fire for too long when it comes to my eating habits, and now it is time to pay the piper. I know where the responsibility lies for what has happened, and I am prepared to do whatever it takes to take care of myself so I can be there for my wife and kids. And when things get tough, I know I have a Savior who can lighten my load, and for that I am truly thankful.

So, for those of you who look forward to my sports posts, I'm not finished opining on the day-to-day of the ball-and-stick games, but I hope you will stick around to read about other happenings. I really enjoy writing about various topics and I appreciate each and every one who takes time out of his or her day to read about what I see through my four eyes. God bless you all and take care of yourself at this most wonderful time of the year.

Chapter 5

Deck Them Halls and All That Stuff

*"For unto you a child is born, unto us a son is given:
and the government shall be upon his shoulder: and his
name shall be called Wonderful, Counsellor, The mighty
God, The everlasting Father, The Prince of Peace."*
Isaiah 9:6, *King James Version*

"That's what Christmas is all about, Charlie Brown."
Linus Van Pelt, *A Charlie Brown Christmas*

I've always loved Christmas. As a matter of fact, I probably go a little overboard when it comes to the Yuletide season. But I can't help it. There is just something about that time of year that makes me feel like a little kid again, and I love that feeling. Now, I'm not one of those Clark Griswold types who over-decorate the house in lights, but I embrace the season and all that comes with it.

Being a Christian, Christmas is one of the two holidays that really puts it all in perspective for me. I find it sad when I hear people say they hate the holidays. My heart really goes out to them. I understand that everyone's circumstances are different, but I can't imagine ever losing my passion for Christmas. Christmas is a time of hope, a time when we are reminded of a birth that changed the world forever. It is a time of love, a time when a Father sent a Son to redeem mankind and to show them the way. It is a time of family, a time when a scared girl and her husband set out on a journey with nothing but each other. It is a time of faith, a time when a miraculous conception was brought to life making anything seem possible. I try my best every year to soak up all that Christmas is for a month so it will be in my heart for the next eleven months.

Throughout the year, I spend a lot of time checking the online stores to see what new Christmas items will be coming out. I have a Christmas movie, music, and book collection that I would put up against anybody's. Beginning with the week of Thanksgiving, I start getting in full-on Christmas mode. Since I'm usually off work the entire Thanksgiving week, I start getting the house decorated on the inside and start playing Christmas music exclusively through New Year's. I try to read as many Christmas books as I can get my hands on. And I'm a sap for any Christmas movie.

Of course, I have my staples that I must listen to or watch throughout the season every single year. It just doesn't feel like Christmas without them. My all-time favorite Christmas carol is "O Holy Night." That song, simply put, is beautiful, powerful, and reverent. It makes me wish I could have been at the stable the night Christ was born. The top of my movie list is *It's a Wonderful Life.* Nothing puts me in the Christmas spirit more than George Bailey banging on Mr. Potter's window and yelling, "Merry Christmas, Mr. Potter!" At school, I always have my students put together a Christmas-themed newspaper titled *The North Pole News.* And that's just the tip of the iceberg.

We also try to squeeze in community activities during this time. We attempt to take the kids to watch a Christmas play, and they usually have some Christmas programs they participate in. Our church has a different program each Sunday throughout the Advent season, and we make sure to attend each one. Central Park in nearby Ashland has a large display called Winter Wonderland of Lights, and we cruise around the park several times during the month and a half they are turned on. It has become tradition for Kristy and I to get coffee and get the kids hot chocolate to drink as we drive around the park pointing out which displays are our favorites. We try to create as many positive memories for the kids to associate with Christmas as possible.

My favorite tradition, however, is the night we open Christmas gifts at our house. The whole family gets in their Christmas pajamas for a family picture on the sofa, and I read the Christmas story to the family as they all sit gathered around me in a circle. That last couple of years Brayden has even helped me read the story which makes the event even more special. Then, we pass out gifts and open them one at a time so everyone can see the gifts each other receives. After we clean up the mess, we make some cookies and pour a glass of milk to leave out for Santa.

You may think this sounds over the top, and maybe it is. All I know is that my family and I enjoy the way we celebrate together, and I would hate to envision a world where there was no Christmas. I always loved the holiday season as a kid, and I want to be able to pass that love on to my kids.

Now, I will admit there have been times I've been overwhelmed and Christmas hasn't gone as I had planned. The Christmas of 2009 was not very enjoyable for my family. Early that December, Kristy's aunt passed away. Then, our three-month-old, Spencer, was put in the hospital for a week with RSV. While in the hospital, Brayden contracted a stomach virus. We shipped Laura-Rae off to stay with the kids' godparents, John and Ruthie Lynd. (I have no idea where we would be without John and Ruthie. They have come through for us in a pinch more than once. I'm not sure they will ever know how much we appreciate and love them.) So you can see how the holiday spirit was quickly slipping away from us. Naturally, it only got worse.

I made arrangements for my mom to come stay with Brayden and Laura-Rae while Spencer was in the hospital. Those plans were dashed when my mom's brother, Jim, was put in the hospital in Jackson the morning she was supposed to leave for our house, and his prognosis wasn't good.

But the cherry on top was when I received a phone call from the hospital. I assumed it was Kristy calling to tell me something, but instead it was the pediatrician. "Mr. Gross? This is Dr. Cook at the hospital. I want you to know that Spencer is fine. He is doing much better. But, Mr. Gross, your wife isn't doing as well. It seems she passed out and dropped Spencer. Like I said, he's just fine. But we're sending her down to the ER to have some tests run."

I was having trouble processing what I was hearing, but eventually I understood what was happening. Kristy, exhausted from staying two nights in the hospital with a sick baby, heard Spencer crying, went to pick him up, and passed out. She crashed into the wall and dropped Spencer on the floor.

I rushed to the hospital on the verge of losing my mind. I had to take Brayden with me, even though he was still sick. When I made it to Spencer's room, they were getting ready to take Kristy downstairs. Thankfully, everything checked out great for her, and they chalked it up to sleep deprivation. We had dodged a major bullet and I was relieved, but I wasn't sure how much more I could take.

The Christmas of 2011 was not quite as bad, but it still wasn't enjoyable. A few days before Christmas, Brayden was put in the hospital with MRSA. He had a nasty-looking infection appear just to the side of his lip. He spent three days in the hospital and they had to do minor surgery to remove the infection. Finally, on the afternoon of Christmas Eve, he was released from the hospital, but the joy of the season had almost been lost. Having gone through two difficult Christmases in three years, and with everything I was dealing with in the fall of 2012, I couldn't help but feel like I was really due for a great Christmas.

December 1-2

By the first weekend in December, we were in full-fledged Christmas mode. My parents had come up for the weekend to visit. They wanted to watch Brayden walk through the Flatwoods Christmas Parade with his Cub Scout pack and Laura-Rae and Spencer the following day in their daycare Christmas program. It was sure to be a busy weekend, but we wouldn't have it any other way.

During my parents' weekend visit, something unexpected happened. Following the parade, we went to the mall to do some shopping. We ate dinner at a restaurant called Fiesta Bravo, a Tex-Mex place that really doesn't have many carb-friendly options. For some reason, I was actually craving to eat there. I was determined to do the best I could, but when I got inside and started eating the chips and salsa, I realized I had a real appetite, something I had lacked for nearly two months. I ordered a chimichanga, fully expecting to only eat half but I wolfed down the whole thing. I was a little worried because it had been several weeks since I had eaten like that. When I checked my sugar level later that night, it was 120; not bad considering what I had eaten.

Over the next couple of days, my appetite continued to flourish. I was very judicious about what I ate to keep from falling back into old habits. I'd worked too hard to let all my progress slip away. Thankfully, the ravenous appetite quickly dissipated, and I was able to not jeopardize the progress I had made. I was pleased the surge had come and gone with little fanfare. Again, I faced and cleared another obstacle. I was beginning to gain confidence with each passing challenge.

December 9-16

As I was hoping for a great Christmas, one week almost ruined the whole season, nearly making it three out of four disastrous holiday seasons. On December 9, a Sunday morning, I was getting Spencer dressed for church. I was sitting on his bed when he bull-rushed me. As usual, I put my hands up late and was unable to catch him before he rammed into me, striking me directly between my spread legs. It hurt, but even more than that, it felt really strange. Something odd had just happened. I finished getting him dressed and hurried to get into the shower so we wouldn't be late. (Just so you know, lateness is a Gross trait. We are often the last ones to arrive, but we are also usually the last to depart). As I was getting ready, I said to Kristy,

"I'm feeling a little weird where Spencer hit me. Something doesn't feel right. It feels like my left nut has been knocked out of place." She just shrugged it off, as did I, and we continued about our morning.

I soldiered on and tried to act like nothing was bothering me, but standing up and sitting down in church was causing me a great deal of discomfort. I was starting to feel sick to my stomach. And then I had a church experience I'm not sure anyone else has ever had. When I stood up to sing the closing hymn, I felt my testicle roll back into place. Talk about a moving experience! I almost shouted, "Hallelujah!" I felt as if I had experienced a genuine Christmas miracle. I soon pushed the event to the back of my mind and assumed that everything was dandy.

Guess what? I was wrong. I felt some lingering soreness and discomfort the rest of the day. Naturally, I assumed it was just a side effect of the direct shot I had taken. Finally, as I was getting up from the couch to go to bed that night, I realized maybe everything wasn't dandy. I could barely walk and my stomach was very queasy. It was all I could do to shuffle to bed and once I laid down, I couldn't get comfortable. I had to get Kristy to help me place pillows under my knees and only then did I feel some relief. Since I was so good at assuming things regarding my health, I figured it would all be better in the morning.

When the alarm clock beeped and my feet hit the floor, I knew that wasn't the case. But I was hoping after moving around some it may get better, like when you have sore muscles. This was clearly not sore muscles, though, because after a few minutes I came back to the bed and told Kristy, "I think I'm going to puke. There's no way I can make it to work today. I'm miserable." I called the urologist and was able to get an appointment just before lunch.

Despite my misery, I managed to take a shower, but that was all I could do. I drove myself to the doctor and as I shuffled into the office, I was pretty sure I looked like I had ridden a horse for the past week. To say the doctor's visit was unpleasant would be like saying the Civil War was a minor skirmish. At least twice the doctor was able to raise me up from the table squalling just by gently touching the afflicted area. After examining me, he said, "You have epididymitis. I'll prescribe an anti-inflammatory and get you scheduled for an ultrasound later today so we can assess the extent of the damage."

For some reason I thought the most embarrassing part of my day was over with but the urology examination paled in comparison to the ultrasound. I took the anti-inflammatory as soon as I got the prescription filled so I was feeling much better by the time I made it to the imaging center. But as I was sitting in the lobby waiting to be called back, I started to panic about the thought of having the ultrasound probe ran over my testicle. I was afraid it would be extremely painful. Thankfully, largely because of my own insecurities, the ultrasound was only humiliating. For some reason, I never expected the imaging technician to be a fifty-five-year-old, motherly woman. I swallowed my pride and hoped for it to be over quickly. Back in May when I had my man-mogram, I couldn't have envisioned a more embarrassing medical dilemma. Funny how quickly things can change.

As the day progressed, I began to feel much better. I was even thinking that going to work the next day was a legitimate possibility. I woke up the next morning feeling better than I had in two days. The only problem was that Laura-Rae was not. She was running a fever and generally not feeling well. Since I get more sick days a year than Kristy, I do most of the sick visits with the kids. As luck would have it, she had the flu. At this point, I was resigning myself to the possibility of never having another Christmas season work out the way I hoped it would. But she's a tough little girl and after a couple of days she bounced back.

She was performing in *The Nutcracker* in a few days, and she didn't want to miss that for any reason.

Total, I missed four days of work that week, but by the end of the week we had not missed anything we had planned on doing, and Laura-Rae and I were both on the mend. My ultrasound showed significant trauma but no major or lasting damage. That week, we took the kids to watch a stage version of *'Twas the Night Before Christmas*, and Kristy and I went to watch John Berry perform his Christmas show as part of her bank Christmas party. And in a week that started with Spencer being the nutcracker, Laura-Rae finished the week by performing a scene from it onstage. All in all, weeks generally don't get more interesting than that.

December 23-January 2

With all the disasters we had faced earlier in the month, the rest of the December couldn't have gone any better and the Gross Family 12 Days of Christmas were in full tilt. It literally seems like we have twelve different days during this time of year in which we are exchanging gifts or going to Christmas parties or participating in some kind of Christmas celebration. And other than Christmas itself, the one thing all of these events have in common is food.

I had survived Halloween because it was so close to my diagnosis that I was scared. Not of monsters, that is, but of eating anything. I owned Thanksgiving because I knew it was just one day. (Actually two because we ate with Kristy's family on the Saturday after Thanksgiving. Thankfully both family meals were not on the same day). But Christmas eating was a different kind of animal. Christmas had sweets upon sweets upon sweets. Everyone loved to make various sweet candies for Christmas, and I loved to eat them. What was I going to do? Resist the temptation, that's what!

When we were at my parents' house, the candies were spread out on the kitchen island just begging for someone to eat them. I knew I wanted some so I budgeted some room for them into my eating plan. I laid off some things I would have normally eaten with Christmas dinner so I could have a few Oreo balls. I had a game plan and I executed it flawlessly. This sweet stuff had nothing on me.

I'd hoped for a great holiday season and it was even better than I could have asked for. The kids had a great time and even got to spend a few extra days in Jackson without us there to get in their way. (We took advantage of that by going to watch *The Hobbit* and treating ourselves to Orange Leaf frozen yogurt.) I would say the Christmas of 2012 was as good as the Christmases of 2009 and 2011 were bad.

And one more personal goal was reached on the final day of the year. I stepped on my scale at home, the one that only registers to 330 pounds, and it said 328. I could now weigh myself at home daily to check my progress. I still used the medical scale at work for my official weight, but being able to weigh at home was a huge deal for me. Upon going back to work on January 2, my official weight was 329, down an amazing forty-eight pounds in just twelve weeks. I was feeling so good about my progress that a few days later I decided to update everyone by blogging about my successful holiday run and to set the table for the new year ahead.

Driven by Faith and Results

When I found out that I was diabetic and was asked to lose 100 pounds in the middle of October, one of the first thoughts I had was, *How am I going to lose any weight with the holidays*

coming up? I mean, there was going to be
Halloween candy, Thanksgiving dinners, and
Christmas. The task seemed all but impossible
in my mind. But as I have been reminded with
my new diagnoses, I know where to turn when
things seem impossible. Luke 1:37 tells us, "For
nothing is impossible with God." And for that, I
am indeed grateful.

I have, at least for the time being, developed a
steely resolve that has allowed me to be extremely
judicious about what I put into my body. I'm very
focused on what I eat and what I choose not
to eat. I have been able to pick my battles and
know when to walk away from something. I have
become so comfortable with my daily diet that I
eat whatever I want, just not always when I want
it or as much as I used to eat of it.

A perfect example of this new lifestyle I have
developed came just last weekend when we were
visiting with my in-laws. My mother-in-law fixed
a nice lasagna which in the past was one of my
favorite dishes. I could easily put away three to
four normal slices (I would usually just eat two
ginormous slices, though) in one sitting; and
then punish the leftovers over the next couple
of days. But, lasagna, and pasta in general, have
become my arch-nemesis, especially if it is not
wheat pasta. The lasagna smelled heavenly but
my stomach turned as I looked at it setting on
the table. At first, I was not going to eat any of
it; I was just going to be content with my salad.
But Kristy talked me into just eating the meat
and sauce and removing the noodles from it. I
was glad I did. Eating the salad and filling of the

lasagna with a slice of garlic bread more than satisfied me, and I was able to avoid unnecessary carbohydrate intake.

Now, there are days when I see something like the lasagna, and I really want to have it but I just have to say no. I have learned how to be comfortable eating most foods I used to gorge myself on, even potato chips, but I'm not there yet with pasta. And that's OK. The new me can take that in stride because I know I'm not alone in dealing with this, and in time I will be able to enjoy pasta again, if only on rare occasions.

Because of the steely resolve I have developed, I have been able to get results much greater than I had anticipated. I set my first weight-loss goal at fifty pounds by the next time I go back to the doctor on January 18. Well, two weeks shy of that date, my weight-loss total stands at forty-eight. I just need to lose two more pounds in two weeks to attain my first goal. (And through a minor Christmas miracle, I managed to lose eighteen pounds from Thanksgiving through New Year's Day, without the benefit of exercise. Unfortunately, the treadmill occupies the spot reserved for the family Christmas tree so my trusty conveyor has been folded up and shoved aside for the last six weeks.) Remarkably, it has not been as difficult as I imagined it would be.

Again, through Him all things are possible and for that I am thankful. I know it sounds cliché, but great things can happen when you truly let go and let God instead of trying to do it on your own. He has placed the right people in my life to help me get through this bump in the road, and the results are keeping me motivated.

Just a few days ago, I decided to try on some old clothes that were in my closet but had not been worn in a few years, or longer. I was thrilled when some size 42 pants and shorts fit comfortably. This made me want to try on a pair of shorts that I wore last summer that were size 48. I was able to slide them on without unbuttoning, unzipping, or squeezing to get into them. I smiled as I thought to myself, *I may need a new wardrobe this summer.*

All in all, I have decided to look as this whole ordeal as a blessing in disguise. I lost seventy-five pounds (eighty if you want to count the five I dropped over spring break in 2009 when I was ravaged with the worst stomach virus I've ever encountered) nearly five years ago and was able to maintain for several months. But I was not able to sustain my progress and began picking up old habits rapidly.

In 1 Corinthians 6:19-20 we are told, "Or do you not know that your body is a temple of the Holy Spirit who is in you, whom you have from God, and that you are not your own? For you have been bought with a price: therefore glorify God in your body." I was most certainly not treating my body as a temple; I was treating it more like a tenement. And while I still have a ways to go in renovating it into that temple, I have fully grasped that I owe it to my wife and kids and those who care about me to treat my body as I should and to set an example for my kids as to what God wants us to be like physically.

I monitor my blood sugar, I take my medications, and I am judicious about what I allow myself to eat. My Lord and Savior has helped narrow my focus and redirect the path of my life and the legacy I leave my kids. I have complete faith I will see this through. I have faced serious challenges in other aspects of my life and I overcame them by becoming more disciplined and focusing on the bigger picture and that is what God has guided me to do. And as long as I have the big picture in my sights, I will not get in God's way as He works His miracle with me. Thanks to all who read and pray for me and may God truly bless you.

Chapter 6

Restoring the Temple

"But as for you, be strong and courageous,
for your work will be rewarded."
2 Chronicles 15:7, *New Living Translation*

"Healing is a matter of time, but it is sometimes
also a matter of opportunity."
Hippocrates

Physical exercise has never been something I particularly enjoy doing. Don't get me wrong. I've always loved to play sports but I just don't do it often enough and never have. One of the reasons is I never wanted to put the work in that was required to be successful. As with so many other things, I found it easier to just make excuses for not playing team sports than it was to put in the necessary work. I was lazy. I can freely admit that now, and I regret being that way.

My favorite sport has always been baseball. When I was growing up playing T-ball and Little League, I worked hard at baseball. I had a passion for the game and knowledge of how to play that was uncanny for a kid my age. As many kids do, I dreamed I would one day play Major League Baseball. I wanted to be like Dale Murphy, Mike Schmidt, and Pete Rose. I wanted to play the game the way they did.

By the third year of Little League, I had found my permanent position: first base. I loved playing first base. Other than pitcher and catcher (both of which I also played), it is the position on the field that is most involved in the game. By this time, I was beginning to put on weight and was already pretty slow. But playing first base was something I felt I was meant to do. I saw it as my job to make sure everyone, especially the infield, knew the game situation and what to do if the ball was hit to them.

But as I got older and entered high school, something happened. I was losing the desire to work as hard at the game I loved. I've never been able to pinpoint what went wrong or why because I still love the game of baseball. I blamed my lack of desire on a coach I had for a few years but that was not fair to him. I didn't particularly enjoy playing for the man, but for me to say it was entirely his fault is ridiculous. More than likely, the most significant factor in my not pursuing my baseball passion was fear of failure. I was simply afraid of not making the team so it was easier not to try and blame it on someone else.

During this time, many of my friends tried to convince me to play football. Both of my brothers had played, and I really enjoyed the game. But I didn't want to put the work in to be successful at it. Unlike my brothers, I didn't like the physical aspect of the game. I wanted to play wide receiver but knew that would never happen. My build was that of a lineman, and I didn't want to play in the trenches. The coach even asked me to play several times, and I seriously gave it some consideration, but it was not for me.

After a few years of doing nothing, I started traveling around the county with some buddies playing games of pickup basketball. We'd been playing in our own neighborhood for a while and decided to branch out because we knew of several different neighborhoods where friends from school would often play. We did this a few years, and it was probably the last time I had my body in decent shape. All that came to an end, however, when my buddies, who were a year ahead of me in school, graduated. That's when my climb up the scale really began.

At the start of my senior year in high school, I weighed 215 pounds. The sad part is that I believed I was absolutely fat. That just gives further evidence the teenage brain doesn't know nearly as much as it thinks it does. I was by no means a svelte, rock-hard athlete, but I was far from what I pictured myself. With a little toning and maintenance, my body would have been fine, but a harsh dose of reality over the next six months really sent me backwards.

Growing up, my dad's side of the family was extremely close. Dad was the oldest of seven kids and all of them had at least two children. We would always gather at Mammaw's and Pappaw's house every fourth Sunday of the month after church for a big potluck dinner. You see, my pappaw was an Old Regular Baptist preacher, and we all went to church where he was the pastor. We had a congregation of between 40-50 people, of which on any given Sunday 90 percent were family. I thought this was the greatest thing in the world when I was little. I had this huge family and we were always doing things together. I may have been young, but I was still savvy enough to understand that not everyone had it as lucky as the Gross family did.

As I found out my senior year of high school, though, things wouldn't always be so utopian for the Grosses. The reality check came when my aunt and uncle announced they were getting divorced. I was seventeen and I knew of people who had divorced, but this wasn't the kind of thing that happened in my family. The Grosses were above that. At least that was the perception I had. For all the great things being raised in a tight-knit, religious family did for me, it came with one major hindrance. It shielded me from the darker side of life and how to handle difficult situations. Terrible things weren't supposed to happen in my family. I didn't understand until then that these things happen in every family and the closer you are, the harder it is to deal with.

The terrible news didn't end with the divorce, though. Much worse news came a few months later when my uncle was diagnosed with a brain tumor. I had lived for seventeen years with this idyllic image of my family and in the course of months it was being shattered. Nothing like this was supposed to happen to us. We lived life the right way, attended church every Sunday, and were as close as any family could be. I mean, bad things don't happen to good people, right?

Of course they do. It's naïve to think that just because you're a "good" person nothing bad will ever happen in your life. I obviously know that now, but at the time this was all happening, it was a startling wake-up call. For the first time in my life I was experiencing a crisis in my faith. How could good, Christian people like my aunt and uncle get a divorce? How could a good, faithful Christian like Uncle John have brain cancer? I'd never had to deal with issues such as these before.

Without realizing it, my whole worldview had changed. I didn't look at things the same. I wasn't as trusting of people. I saw more bad in things than I saw good. Prayer was not as comforting as it once had been. So I turned to food. Food provided comfort that I was getting from nowhere else. By the time I graduated from high school, I was up to 250 pounds. I had gained thirty-five pounds over the course of the school year. I had become sedentary, my eating habits were atrocious, and my weight was now becoming a major concern. But as with most things, I just brushed it off and thought, *No big deal.*

That was the way I usually dealt with adversity when I was younger. I wouldn't open myself up to anyone about anything. I just kept it inside. There were times people knew when stuff was bothering me, but I would just deflect, ignore, and avoid. I was intensely private and wanted to keep it that way. I could shield my feelings as well as anybody, and when it was too hard I would just slip away for some solitude.

My first three semesters of college at Morehead State University were great. I somehow managed to not gain more weight, but by the last semester of my sophomore year, something changed. Again, I have never pinpointed what caused the major shift, but I was no longer inspired by school. I had just come off a semester where I had my best GPA to date and followed that up with a 1.0 GPA and lost my partial scholarship. I spun my wheels for the next few semesters, and I began to pack on the pounds. I was depressed and hurting, and I was trying to hide that from everybody who cared about me.

Thankfully, unlike so many who are experiencing what I was at the time, I didn't turn to drugs or alcohol as my escape. I'm not sure if it was my Old Regular Baptist upbringing or just fear of what those things could do to my life, but I chose to turn to food instead. It was perfect. Mom was a great cook, I liked to eat, I despised physical activity, and there was just something euphoric about stuffing my face. And I usually didn't discriminate about what I foundered on either. Potato chips, ice cream, cheeseburgers, hot wings, French fries, cake, pudding, pies, country breakfasts, etc., etc., etc. What could be better than that smorgasbord?

My laziness and apathy subsided after three semesters, and I finally decided what I needed to do to graduate and my focus was renewed. The problem was I had gained another thirty-five pounds and my eating habits hadn't changed. Through the grace of God, and one really lenient science professor, I graduated from Morehead State in the fall of 2000. I had a government degree but no desire to go to law school or to teach. In other words, I didn't have a very practical degree for employment. But, as you would naturally suspect, I did have the right degree to be a financial advisor.

Three months after I graduated, I had my first career and, as short-lived as it was, I learned many valuable lessons from my first job post-college. The first lesson was that I'm no salesman, and I have no desire to ever try to be one. The second lesson was that sometimes you have to find out things on your own; it's the best way to learn. After quitting, my dad told me one day, "I never could figure out why you wanted that job. It didn't seem like it was the right fit for you." I responded with, "Well, you could have told me that before I took the job." Ever the one to dispense sage advice, he replied, "It was better for you to find out on your own." I've thought about those words many times, and I realized he was right.

Perhaps the greatest lesson I learned by taking that job can be summed up by the title of the classic country song by Dan Seals, "Everything That Glitters Is Not Gold." Boy, ain't that the truth! I bought into the high life that some of the guys at the office were living and bit the sales pitch that was given me in the interview process hook, line, and sinker. But after three months of driving to Lexington from Jackson and back home, shelling out the cash for licensing exams, and getting a loan from my folks for a new wardrobe, I was in the hole. In a short period of time, I actually lost money. And friends and family that I dearly love avoided me like the plague when I asked to come talk to them on a sales call. I had no intention of really selling them anything; I just needed referrals and experience.

Some good did come from this experience, though. Working every day in a professional environment gave me a confidence boost. I was feeling better about myself and wanted to look and dress the part. During my three-month career as a financial planner, I lost fifteen pounds. It was the first time I had shed any weight in nearly four years. I was on the right track, but as happened so often, I was easily derailed.

After quitting, many of the familiar feelings I had experienced midway through college began to resurface. To look at me wallowing in my self-pity, you would have thought I was the first person to ever quit a job he wasn't suited for. (Actually, I was suited for it. I had to wear a suit every day. Ba-Dum-Bum!) I was desperately searching for a purpose in my life. I knew I was supposed to do something but I had no idea what it was or where to find it. I would lie in bed during the wee hours of morning and beg God to set me on the right path. I would seriously consider packing a few things and just leaving while Mom and Dad were asleep and call them when I got to St. Louis or Wilmington, N.C., or wherever I was thinking about at the time. But I couldn't do that to them. The thought of starting over in a place foreign to me with no one to help me find a job or a place to live was frightening, but the thought of ripping my parents' hearts out was more than I could bear.

One night shortly after my twenty-third birthday, I decided to join the Marines. I filled out an application online. I still don't know why I did that, but a few weeks later, a recruiter called to talk to me. I was home alone and for some reason, I didn't answer the phone. I heard the recruiter leaving a message for me to call him back. I was panic-stricken and deleted the message. Part of me really wanted to enlist and see what I was made of, but the rest of me wouldn't allow it. I was badly out of shape and had gained back all the weight I had recently lost, plus a few extra, and was not sure I would be able to pass the physical to get into the Marine Corps. But the overriding factor was the fear of telling Mom that I had enlisted. I once mentioned joining the ROTC in college for the additional scholarship but Mom would have none of it. She knew what it was like to send a husband overseas, and she wanted no part of doing the same with a child.

As it turned out, I don't believe God ever intended for me to join the military. A few weeks after receiving the call from the recruiter, terrorists attacked the World Trade Center and the Pentagon. The world all of us were living in was forever changed. I couldn't help but think that I nearly drove to Louisville a few weeks prior to have a physical and sign paperwork to enlist. The thought was sobering because I had never considered the possibility of an attack on American soil and the repercussions that would follow. I was just looking to have a career and maybe travel the world, but being involved in a war that may never end was not on my radar. Part of me was relieved that I didn't go to visit the recruiter; the other part was ashamed because I knew I didn't have what it takes to be in the military. I've always admired all the men and women who served and literally laid their lives on the line for us to enjoy the freedoms we all too often take for granted. After September 11, 2001, my admiration and respect for these individuals has grown immensely.

As I mentioned earlier, though, I don't think it was in God's plans for me to enlist in the military. After 9/11, I knew I needed to quit feeling sorry for myself and get my butt in gear. I was hired to be a substitute teacher while I went back to school once again to figure out what I wanted to do with my life. The one thing I said when I entered college out of high school was I didn't want to be a teacher. After substitute teaching for a month, I realized that was exactly what I wanted to do. So, after a little more than a year of learning about life in the real world, I once again enrolled in college, this time with a defined career path. While everything in my life seemed to be changing constantly, there was one thing that didn't: I was eating every meal as if it was going to be my last. My dietary and exercise habits were appalling and even though I knew what I was doing to my body, I didn't care.

Not long after I started back to school, Morehead State announced it was starting a new graduate program for people who wanted to come back and get a teaching degree. I took this to be a sign I made the right decision and I applied to get into the program. Several months passed and I never heard anything so I assumed I didn't get in. I would soon discover, though, that was not a bad thing as I was once again facing a life-changing event that interrupted my studies and completely turned my life upside down.

New Year's Eve 2002 is a night that will always live in infamy in my memory. About mid-afternoon, my mom answered the phone, and I could tell the news was upsetting. When she hung up, she told me that my cousin, Brad, who had been battling cancer for the better part of a year, was not doing well. The doctors had found several more lumps and the cancer was now on his spine. He was in the hospital. After taking time to pray and compose myself, I knew what I needed to do. I packed a bag with some clothes and a few toiletries and told my mom, "I'm going to Ashland, and I don't know when I'll be back." As I walked to my car, the Lord was telling me this was what I was meant to do, and Mom and I both knew as I left home that evening, I would never again live in the house I grew up in.

Brad only lived four more months. I moved in with him and his wife to help take care of him during the day. Doing so kept his wife from having to quit her job. Those months were excruciating, but I wouldn't trade them for anything in the world. You see, Brad was more than a cousin; he was like my third brother. We'd grown up together, gone to school together, and even lived with each other for three years while at Morehead State. He was the one person in the world that really understood me. Losing him was like losing part of my soul.

Yet, through all of this, something really odd seemed to be happening in my life. My life was beginning to take shape. I was beginning to see the path my life was following, and it was certainly not one I had ever dreamed of traveling. It was definitely being guided by a divine hand. If I had been successful as a financial advisor, I wouldn't have had the opportunity to be there for my best friend, my cousin, my brother. If I had joined the military, I wouldn't have been able to take a semester off school and take care of Brad. If I had been accepted to the graduate program when I first applied, I couldn't have dropped out to do what was necessary.

During the time I was taking care of Brad, however, I finally received a letter saying I was accepted to the Masters of Arts in Teaching program at Morehead State University for the fall semester of 2003. But that wasn't all. Brad's wife, Kristy, and I had gone through an experience in which the two of us were the only ones who understood the kind of hell the other had lived through. Even though we had known each other for more than fifteen years, our relationship had changed. I was compelled to take care of her and in so doing, we fell in love. My life now had a defined course for the first time. I am convinced all the things that had happened in my life were leading to this. Where I could see dead ends, God saw my future.

I know rehashing these events of my life has gotten longwinded and many may be asking, "What does this have to do with your physical condition?" I'm just trying to provide insight to some significant events in my life and where my downward slope with gluttony began. As with most things, they are not quickly built or destroyed. A brand-new building takes years, even decades, to fall into disrepair. A car body deteriorates over time. In both instances, the withering is more rapid when the building or car is not being properly maintained. The human body is the same way.

From the time I was seventeen until I was thirty-four, I was not maintaining my body; therefore, my health was disintegrating. What had first started as food therapy when I was feeling depressed became a way of life. Once my life found the proper direction, I was gluttonous in good times and bad. I had taken something that was intended to maintain and strengthen my body and was using it for destruction. I was smart enough to know what I was doing, but unwilling to accept responsibility for it.

The good news, though, was that my body was not so dilapidated that it needed torn down. It needed a major overhaul, but it wasn't as bad as it could have been. After two and a half months of eating much healthier, it was time to finally start the renovations. Once the Christmas tree finally came down on January 6, it was time to start restoring the temple on January 7.

January 7-17

Returning to the treadmill was going to be huge commitment for me. Not being a fan of exercise, I have learned laziness and physical activity are not BFFs; therefore, me and exercise would be like oil and water, Montagues and Capulets, Wolverines and Buckeyes. We just don't mix. But the days of making excuses and taking the easy way out were over. If I wanted to reach my ultimate goal, I couldn't avoid exercise so I made the conscious decision to embrace it. I was going to meet the treadmill head-on, and I was going to win.

In my head I devised a workout plan. If I could get on the treadmill four days during the week and walk at least 40 minutes each time, that would be a great start. My first day getting back in action was Monday, January 7. I was just hoping to survive and see how my body responded. I followed that up with a session on Tuesday and then again on Wednesday. I wanted to come out of the gates strong. The only problem was my body wasn't ready for three days in a row, but that was OK. I persevered and, even though my times weren't as good, I completed my sessions.

It was after walking on the third day that I was inspired to create a spreadsheet to chart how far I was walking, how quickly I was walking, and how many calories I was burning. I knew if I were to keep a record of this information I would be much more likely to continue walking. I must admit I have a fascination with stats and have since I was a young child. I would stare at the statistics on the back of baseball cards for hours on end trying to memorize a player's career numbers. I learned to calculate earned run average and batting average as soon as I could multiply and divide. Throughout school, I learned to compartmentalize things in my mind by using numbers. Most of the time I can remember numbers precisely yet I cannot do the same with words (and you can forget asking me to quote song lyrics or movie one-liners). I've always had a connection with numbers, so it only made sense to track my progress on the treadmill by keeping a chart to compare numbers each day I walked.

From January 7-17, I was on the treadmill seven times, and I could already see progress. I had knocked more than ninety seconds off my one-mile time. But there was one funny thing happening. I was weighing daily now and was trying to drop a pesky two pounds before returning to the doctor on January 18. I'd been stuck at 329 for two weeks despite my new efforts to exercise. I had finally hit the proverbial wall at the worst possible time. I'd been fortunate for twelve weeks and had shed weight easily, but here I was a day away from my second doctor's visit, and I was struggling to reach my weight-loss goal of fifty pounds. What had seemed like a sure thing was now looking highly doubtful.

January 18

Since leaving the doctor's office on October 18, three months earlier, I had been looking forward to this day. I knew I had made progress, but I was eager to see the numbers and talk with Dr. Connett to see if there was anything I was doing that needed modified. But the real reason I was looking forward to this day had nothing to do with my health. Laura-Rae, my sweet, matter-of-fact, unassuming, wise-beyond-her-years daughter, was turning five, and three of her best friends were coming over to our house for a sleepover. She was looking forward to it, Kristy was giddy planning all the things they were going to do, and I was apprehensive about being outnumbered 5 to 1 by girls. (We shipped Brayden and Spencer over to stay with John and Ruthie for the night.) In order to handle the night ahead, I was in desperate need of a good doctor's report or otherwise I would mentally check out for the night.

Fortunately, my prayers were answered, and I couldn't have been more thankful. Dr. Connett was very pleased by my results. I still had work to do but she was encouraged. I could feel a sense of relief wash over me. I had put in a lot work to change my physical condition and it was paying off. (You have to look at the numbers in Appendix A to believe the difference.)

The only problem was I'd failed to reach my goal of losing fifty pounds. I was stuck at forty-nine and even though I was a little disappointed, I couldn't have been happier. The feeling I had leaving the doctor's office that day was significantly different than the previous two times I had left there. I went home and said another word of prayer, but this time it was a prayer of thanks and a prayer for the resolve to keep going, to not rest on my laurels, but to continue to the finish line.

As I was making soup and helping Laura-Rae and her friends make their own personal pizzas, I truly felt blessed. It was for moments such as this, moments where lasting memories were being created, that made my journey worth all the work. The following day, after all the girls had been returned to their parents, I reflected on what the past three months had been like and what I hoped the next three would be like. The one pervading thought that would not go away was, *Even though I hadn't met my goal, I hadn't failed.* That's when I started looking at new goals for the next three months and for the rest of the year. I was focused and determined and was positive all the goals I had set would be attained. I once again sat down to inform my readers of my latest results and to share a little perspective on my progress.

Sometimes Not Reaching a Goal
Does Not Mean You Failed

Yesterday was the day I had been waiting for since finding out I had diabetes. It was my first three-month follow-up to see how much progress I had made. I had set my goal for weight-loss at fifty pounds, a goal I was not sure was actually attainable. But as of two weeks ago, I would have bet a large sum that there was no way I would fall short of that goal. I was down forty-eight pounds at that time and figured losing two more pounds in two weeks would be a lock. Well, despite more exercise and better eating habits, I hit the proverbial wall and only lost one more pound over that time, bringing my total to forty-nine. I was a little disappointed, but I was able to recognize the fact that there are some times when just because you don't reach a goal, it doesn't mean you failed. I was 98 percent of the way to reaching my goal, but the fact that I dropped nearly fifty pounds in three months is astounding and has done wonders for my body. The proof of what the weight-loss has done for me is in the sugar-free pudding.

This trip to the doctor was immensely better than the last few times I had been. My doctor summed it up best when she said, "It's always more enjoyable when you get good news from the doctor." Amen to that, sister. Now for the results. My liver function has improved greatly. There are two levels they measure and both need to be below 40. I dropped one from the high 70s to the low 30s and the other from the 140 range to 47, nearly within acceptable range.

My sugar was 115, cut nearly in half, and as result I only have to take my Metformin pill once a day now instead of twice. One of the best results, however, was my A1C hemoglobin test. I don't know all the particulars of this test but it gives a 3-4-month measure of the sugar level in your hemoglobin. If your number is over 6.5, you are diabetic. In October, mine was 7.9. Yesterday, it was 5.8, just 0.2 away from being back in the normal range. The best news, though, was that she said when I lose fifteen more pounds, I can quit taking the Metformin altogether and see how my body responds to that. Things are definitely looking better than they did three months ago.

As always, I know who has helped me achieve these results, and I am entirely grateful for the presence of Jesus Christ in my life. After giving my post-holiday update a few weeks ago, a friend sent me a few tweets with Bible verses in them. One was James 1:6 and the other was Matthew 7:7-11. Both scriptures center on not being afraid to ask God for guidance. It's hard to receive things if you don't ask for them. When I came home from my doctor's visit on October 10, I did a lot of praying and asking, and I have received. But, I did not sit around and just expect things to happen without putting in the work myself. The Lord wasn't going to magically wave a wand and allow me to instantly start dropping weight and lower my numbers while I ate whatever I wanted to stuff into my face. That's not how it works. He helped me to gain the strength and focus to put the work in to get the results I needed and even though I came up one pound shy of my goal, I have not failed.

As for goals, I have a new goal set for the next three-month follow-up and one for the rest of the year. By the time I go back to the doctor in late April, I want to be down another 25 pounds. As for the yearlong goal, I want to walk 365 miles on the treadmill this year and burn 35,000 calories while doing so. Over the past two weeks, I've been able to walk nearly 17 miles while burning 1800 calories. To put that in perspective, if I achieve this goal, the distance I will have walked on the treadmill would be equivalent to walking from my house in Russell, Ky., to my brother's house in Sweetwater, Tenn., and then walk from his house back to Knoxville. As for burning that many calories, it would be the equivalent of burning off two weeks' worth of meals. While those goals seem lofty at first glance, I feel there is no way I will fall short of them. Unlike the weight-loss, which you can only control to an extent, I can totally control how often I exercise and for how long I do it. Besides, Philippians 4:13 tells us, "I can do all things through Christ, because He gives me strength." So, phase one of my temple restoration is nearly complete, and I encourage any who read this to follow suit. It is never too late to do good for yourself or God. Until next time, thanks for reading and God bless!

Mom, Dad, and me on my wedding day

Master's degree graduation, May 2005.

Brayden and me at Busch Gardens, 2007

Niagara Falls, 2006

With Brayden at Disney World, 2007

At Brayden's T-Ball game, 2010

Christmas 2011

At Brayden's baseball practice, Spring 2012.

With the kids, Easter 2012.

With Greg, Spring 2012

With Spencer, Summer 2012

With Dad, Fall 2012

With Brayden at Giants vs. Bengals, November 2012

My first 5K, May 2013

With Laura-Rae, Summer 2013

With Mom and Dad, Summer 2013

At Dodgers vs Braves playoff game, October 2013

Before the Monster Mash 5K, October 2013

Crossing the Monster Mash finish line, October 2013

With the kids, Thanksgiving 2013

Christmas 2013

With Brayden, January 2014

Chapter 7

Can't Take the Pain

*"And the God of all grace, who called you to his eternal glory
in Christ, after you have suffered a little while, will himself
restore you and make you strong, firm, and steadfast."*
1 Peter 5:10, *New International Version*

"One good thing about music, when it hits you, you feel no pain."
Bob Marley

I think it's safe to say most people don't enjoy experiencing physical pain. Now, I know there are some people who say they do, but joy is not a normal response to actual agony. I know anytime I'm in pain, I'm not happy about it. Thankfully, I haven't had any prolonged periods of excruciating pain, but I have had several nagging injuries.

The first time I can really remember being in pain was when I was in third grade. I'm sure I had painful things happen before then, but how they happened or what they were never stuck with me the way this incident has. One day near the end of the school year I was returning to my seat and someone pulled my chair out from underneath me. I crashed down onto the floor . . . HARD! I have no idea who did it or why, but all I knew then, and know now is that it hurt . . . BAD! I didn't go to the doctor to be examined but I'm pretty sure I badly bruised my coccyx. (If you have to ask what that is, then you've probably never bruised or broken your tailbone.) The worst part was I had baseball practice that night and wasn't sure I was going to be able to move. I caught a break when practice was canceled, and I didn't have to suffer through the pain that night because not practicing wasn't an option in my young mind. As a result, I still have trouble with my lower back.

The longest duration of physical pain I've ever had was when I sprained my ankle my freshman year of high school. I was playing an intense game of pickup hoops at my neighbor's house when I drove baseline for a layup. It was a move I'd made hundreds of times, sometimes successfully making the shot, but most often bricking it. I can't say for sure whether I made the shot this time because when I landed I barely caught the asphalt, which was about six inches higher than the gravel, and rolled my ankle. The pain was awful, and I couldn't put any weight on it. Thanks to my buddies Duker and Wendal, who each lent me a shoulder to lean on, I was able to hobble the short distance down the road to get back home. Mom and

Dad took me to the ER, and the X-ray revealed a nasty sprain. The next morning, my ankle had swollen to my knee and my leg was about twelve different colors, none of which were pretty. Again, the worst part about it was that baseball season was just beginning. It took about three months to completely get over the injury, but to this day I have a limited range of motion in my right ankle.

And then there was the time I went squirrel hunting with my brother Greg at our uncle Jim's house the day before Thanksgiving. We were both in college so we were on break from classes, and for some reason I thought it would be a good idea to go hunting with him. I've never really enjoyed hunting, mostly because it seems like a lot of work, and it usually means you have to get up too early. Well, I should've stayed in bed this day for sure. After several hours wandering through the woods and not laying eyes on any squirrels, we were ready to call it a day. Just as we were about to leave, I could feel a thumping in my chest and heard what sounded like a fleet of helicopters buzzing by overhead. I was startled by the unexpected noise and looked up to see a covey of quail passing over us. Once we regained our composure, Greg thought it would be a good idea to track them. Naturally, it sounded like a good idea to me so we started down a slight incline toward a thicket where we thought the birds were taking cover.

A few steps down the hill, I stepped on a branch that was hidden underneath the wet leaves causing me to slip. The full weight of my body landed on my elbow, which subsequently jammed my shoulder. I was writhing in agony, and every time I tried to sit up, the pain in my shoulder forced me back down to the ground. I asked Greg, "Can you help me up?" It was then I realized he was doubled over and shaking, but not out of sympathy for his baby brother lying on the ground. He was laughing uncontrollably! And he continued to do so until we made it back to his house. The shoulder only hurt for about two weeks, and there was no significant damage to it, but I did learn a couple of things. One, the shoulder is instrumental in sitting up when you are lying down, and when you have a bum shoulder it's very difficult to perform that basic function. Second, when the chips are down, I can always count on Greg . . . to laugh at me. Needless to say, I haven't been hunting since.

Some physical pains don't come from injury, though. Sometimes uric acid can build up in your joints and give you a raging case of something called gout. Gout is very painful when the afflicted joint gets inflamed and even the slightest touch of a bedsheet can cause intolerable pain. I thought I had broken my toe the first time my gout flared up. One night I was sitting on the couch with my leg propped up and Kristy, wanting to sit down beside me, grabbed my toe to move my foot. I screamed a few things I had to repent for later, and she said, "I thought it was your other foot." I felt bad about that, but pain makes you do crazy things.

The worst gout incident came when Brayden was about eighteen months old. We were in Jackson visiting the family when my accursed affliction decided to rear its ugly head. I was sitting on the couch at my parents' house when Brayden came rumbling toward me the way only a thirty-pound toddler can. I was in the midst of trying to move my foot when he tripped over a pillow on the floor and delivered a double axe handle to my left big toe that would have made Hacksaw Jim Duggan proud. I've never experienced a burst of pain like that in my life. I didn't know whether to laugh, cry, puke, or do all three. Brayden was freaked out, I was miserable, and I'm sure Greg was somewhere laughing.

Although these things caused some physical pain, they all healed and I have no lasting complications. The same cannot be said for emotional pains. Even though we can't see emotional scars, everyone has them, and those tend to linger much longer than physical ones. I talked about some of my emotional scars in the previous chapter so I won't burden you with rehashing them again, but I would like to mention that besides prayer, one way I deal with emotional pain is by listening to music.

Music has the power to heal. There's a song for just about every situation someone has gone through, is going through, or will go through in life. Songs have a way of speaking to us individually. When a lyricist writes a personal song, she pours her own experiences into it. When a vocalist makes the hairs on your neck and arms stand on end, he is unleashing his own raw emotions. Music is mentioned throughout the Bible so I have no qualms in saying music is a powerful tool that God has placed in our lives for a reason. The most important function of music is that it should be used to praise God and to worship Him, but I believe He also placed it in our lives because one song can provide healing for an abundance of people at the same time.

Occasionally, as I look back on my life, I have often wondered how cool it would be to make a mix CD of the songs that mean something to me. More or less, it would be a soundtrack of my life. The first song I ever remember hearing that really stirred something in me was George Strait's "Amarillo by Morning." I was probably only six or seven at the time but I knew the song was emotional and personal. I have been a huge George Strait fan ever since. Another song that spoke volumes to me the first time I heard it was Bon Jovi's "Thank You For Loving Me." Upon hearing it, I realized that was the song I wanted to dance to with my bride on my wedding day and sure enough, when Kristy and I got married, we danced to that song.

Then there are songs you can hear hundreds of times and, even though you really like those songs, they may not speak to you on a deeper level. All of sudden, one day, you hear a particular song during a special circumstance, and it instantly becomes a song to add to your soundtrack. I've experienced that phenomenon twice. The first was the Beatles "Let it Be." That has always been my favorite song by the Fab Four, but it took on a whole new meaning when the doctor was playing it in the delivery room when Brayden was born. I can't hear that song now without getting emotional and thinking about Brayden. The other is Aerosmith's "Don't Want to Miss a Thing." Again, this was my favorite song by them, but the meaning of the song changed forever when it was playing during Spencer's birth. (Unfortunately, Laura-Rae doesn't have a delivery day song like the boys because the doc who delivered her didn't play anything in the operating room. However, I have adopted the George Strait song "I Saw God Today" for her.)

Perhaps the most unexpected song I would add to my soundtrack blindsided me on the treadmill. It was a song I'd heard many times before and thought it was great. But on this day, it became significant in my life and in my weight-loss journey.

January 26

Three weeks had passed since I'd made a concentrated effort to start exercising, and I was seeing the results of my work. I'd only lost one pound the first two weeks of exercising, but I had knocked a little more than four minutes off my two-mile time. Then, during the third week, I lost four pounds and was feeling pretty good about what I had been doing. My times were still pretty consistent, but I was burning more and more calories and feeling more confident about the exercise. I felt as if I was putting in some good work, but that I hadn't really challenged myself. And when I started running on the treadmill on January 26, I expected it to be my ordinary forty-minute walk in which I burned in the neighborhood of 300 calories. That was until I heard the song.

I was approaching the thirty-minute mark of my workout when I realized if I pushed a little harder I would be able to lay down two miles in less than half an hour for the first time. I planned to cruise the last ten minutes because I was beginning to feel fatigued but when I heard Third Day's song, "I Can't Take the Pain" come on my iPod, I knew God was speaking to me. For those of you who aren't familiar with the song, I suggest you make yourself familiar with it immediately. It has long been one of my favorite Third Day songs, but on this day, it was as if I was hearing the words for the first time.

The song is sung from the perspective of Peter as he denies Christ three times before the Crucifixion. Lead singer Mac Powell's soulful, Southern voice lends to the anguish Peter experiences as he turns his back on Christ in His hour of need. The song is very emotional and gut-wrenching, and as I was gearing down to coast the rest of the way, a voice was telling me, "Push through the pain. Go for it." I started to think about what Peter must have gone through during those agonizing hours of Christ's persecution and execution and how a little fatigue from running paled in comparison. My heart began to break as I was running and tears began to roll down my cheeks. I started thinking about times I had turned my back on Christ, and let me tell you, it was a lot more than three. I was being convicted as I ran, and I started to feel like Forrest Gump. So I just ran, and ran some more.

Once the song finished I was filled with a new determination. I was going to push myself as far as I could go. I had a renewed focus and I wasn't going to be denied. My time was by no means great, but my sense of accomplishment was overwhelming when I finished a 5K on the treadmill in 48:43. Before this day, I had set a goal to compete in some 5Ks, but I was not really sure I had it in me to complete one. Now, after just twelve days of running, I had finished one. The feeling was amazing. God spoke to me through a song and gave me the shot of confidence I needed.

As an added bonus, I burned more than 500 calories during my workout for the first time. I was on my way to bigger and better things. I just needed to keep up the momentum. My hard work was paying dividends and that just made me want to work harder. For the first time in a long time, I felt as if I was on top of the world and nothing was going to stop me from reaching my goals.

March 3

Over the next several weeks I was able to continue the roll I had been on. At no point in my adult life had I ever been in such an exercise groove. I was transforming my life and it was awesome. I'd traded in my old, destructive habits for new, constructive ones. My attitude toward working out and getting in shape was foreign to me at first, but with each passing day it became more natural. From January 26 through February 27, I completed four more 5Ks on the treadmill and knocked four and a half minutes off my original time. I even completed one of those varying the incline of the treadmill, which was quite an accomplishment for me.

During February, I noticed two things. I spent most of the winter freezing my tail off. I wasn't sure if I had lost so much of my insulation that I was having a hard time staying warm or if it was the medication. As it turns out, it was the Metformin. I had cut back to only taking one pill a day and, even though February was no warmer than January, I was able to keep my internal temperature much more regulated. Cold weather had never really bothered me, but after spending most of the winter feeling like a popsicle, I was ready for milder temperatures.

The other thing I noticed was the number of compliments I was receiving from people whom I saw nearly every day. Many co-workers were taking notice of how much weight I had lost and were going out of their way to let me know they had noticed. Parents of my children's friends were stopping me at daycare or birthday parties to congratulate me on my weight-loss. Fellow congregants at church were doing the same. I was overwhelmed by the support of the people around me. As they talked to me, they always had a gleam in their eyes, and they seemed to be genuinely happy for me. The congratulatory pats and kind words made me feel great and really showed me how much people were paying attention. It made me think of the line that Clarence the Angel writes to George Bailey at the end of *It's a Wonderful Life*: "Remember George: No man is a failure who has friends."

But through the compliments and the well-wishes, one question people would ask constantly nagged at me. What's the secret? I usually brushed the question off and answered it with, "I just eat right and exercise. It's as simple as that." But the more I thought about it, the more I realized there really was more to it. On the evening of March 3, I decided to address how I was successfully changing my life and my habits in a blog.

Giving Credit Where Credit Is Due

I'm approaching the five-month mark of living a healthier lifestyle. I must admit, it has been remarkably easier than I anticipated. I guess having your back to a wall has a way of doing that to you. I'm now down sixty-three pounds and have gotten on the treadmill four times a week for the past eight weeks. As a matter of fact, I've gotten so used to doing the treadmill that I actually make plans around my exercise instead of making excuses to not do it. I never thought I'd see the day when I'd get cranky because I hadn't had my cardio. I guess investing in a treadmill last summer, even though it was barely used for several months, was worth the cost after all.

Over the course of the last month, people have really begun noticing the transformation my body is undergoing. I've had countless people make comments about my weight-loss and several who continually ask me about my progress. I have to confess, it feels amazing that people have noticed and are taking an interest in how I am doing. Many have even offered words of encouragement and admiration for what I have been able to do thus far. While I have spent most of my life trying to not really be noticed and trying to keep personal details personal, I have found being open and discussing what I am going through to be cathartic and necessary to being successful in reaching my goals. After all, if people are taking enough interest to notice how I am changing my body, the least I can do is be open about things.

Perhaps the question that is most often asked of me nowadays is, "How are you doing it?" (One person asked me, "So, what's your secret?" I resisted the urge to say, "Diabetes. It's worked wonders for me.") I always tell them the answer is simple: I'm eating more nutritiously and exercising regularly. I know that doesn't sound flashy but it's true. But after being asked that question again a few days ago, I began to think about how I'd actually done it. The answer I had been giving was true, but, honestly, there is more to it than that. When I say diet and exercise, I'm leaving out the most important part: God. If not for Him, none of this would be possible. So, upon further reflection of how God has guided me through this time, I have pinpointed several keys to what has allowed me to be successful in restoring my body and rebuilding my relationship with God.

1) **Faith**: This is where it all starts for me. While I have always had faith in the Holy Trinity, I had gotten to a point in my life where I was relying more on myself than I was on the Father, Son, and Holy Spirit. When you trust yourself more than the Trinity, that's when you get yourself in trouble. After getting the dickens scared out of me in October, my eyes were quickly opened and I knew immediately where I needed to put my faith if I was going to be successful in changing my life. Jesus tells us in Matthew 17:20, "I tell you the truth, if your faith is as big as a mustard seed, you can say to this mountain, 'Move from here to there,' and it will move. All things will be possible for you." I needed to move a mountain, or (more aptly) remove a mountain of weight from the frame of my body, and I knew I couldn't do it alone. I chatted with God about getting that done, and we've been in constant communication since. If you're looking for a place to start, try renewing your faith in the King of Kings.

2) **Attitude**: If you're to be successful in anything you do, you must have a positive attitude. A colleague of mine often tells his students and players, "Whether you think you can or can't, you're right either way." Henry Ford is credited

with the original quote but it makes a lot of sense to me. If you expect to fail, you will. If you expect to succeed, you will do that, too. So, I approach every day determined to be successful. I don't just sit around waiting for things to happen; I make them happen. Luke 12:35 tells us to "be dressed, ready for service and keep your lamps burning" and that is exactly how I have approached my situation. I feel God has plans for me, and in order for those plans to be carried out, I need to stay positive and keep the determination to follow God where He leads me.

3) **Desire**: In *Harry Potter and the Sorcerer's Stone*, Harry encounters a unique mirror that lets him see his family who had been killed years earlier. Harry continues to sneak around to get a peek at the mirror whenever possible. Eventually Professor Dumbledore tells Harry about why everyone who looks into the mirror sees something different. He tells Harry, "It shows us nothing more or less than the deepest, most desperate desire of our hearts." After getting my wakeup call in the fall, I took a look into my own personal Mirror of Erised and saw that I wanted to be around for Kristy, Brayden, Laura-Rae, and Spencer for as long as I possibly could. I want to celebrate milestone anniversaries and birthdays and get to know my grandchildren. This wasn't going to be possible going down the road I had been traveling, so now I'm traveling a much better road. Psalm 37:4 says, "Take delight in the Lord, and He will give you your heart's desires." That sounds pretty good to me so that is what I intend to do.

4) **Ownership**: I've taken ownership of the problem at hand because I couldn't resolve my problems if I wasn't willing to admit that I had them or that I was at fault in creating them. I knew I had a genetic predisposition to be diabetic, but I had taken that too lightly for too long. No one to blame but myself. 1 Timothy 5:8 sums it up pretty well. "But if anyone does not provide for his relatives, especially for members of his household, he has denied the faith and is worse than an unbeliever." I don't want to be worse than an unbeliever, but I do want to provide for my family so that means I must take ownership of the problem and take steps to correct it, and I have. Going through life ignoring problems and pretending they don't exist is not a solution, and to me, it's not an option. Own them, solve them, praise the Lord, and move on. Simple as that.

These keys have proven to be life-changing for me, and I would recommend anyone who is facing a similar issue to follow them. What do you have to lose? Me, I had a lot to lose if I didn't change, and I'll bet you do, too. Recently, I read a book on desire by John Eldredge* and in it he says, "Life is not a problem to be solved; it is an adventure to be lived." I reflected upon that statement and my life. Too often when we face problems, we let them dominate our lives. It's easy to do. But what we really need to do is view them as bumps on the road of the journey we are on. Sometimes we may have to take the long way around when we wanted to take the shortcut, but the classic Robert Frost** poem puts that in perspective for us:

"Two roads diverged in a wood, and I,

I took the one less traveled by,

And that has made all the difference."

Desire: The Journey We Must Take to Find the Life God Offers by John Eldredge

**"The Road Not Taken" by Robert Frost

Chapter 8

Revival

*"Create in me a clean heart, O God, and
renew a right spirit within me."*
Psalm 51:10, *English Standard Version*

*"The story of Christian reformation, revival, and renaissance
underscores that the darkest hour is often just before the dawn, so we
should always be people of hope and prayer, not gloom and defeatism.
God the Holy Spirit can turn the situation around in five minutes."*
Os Guinness

There is something magical about springtime in Eastern Kentucky. After the leaves change color and fall to the ground in October, we spend the next four to five months in a colorless, drab surrounding. Don't get me wrong; I love winter. As a matter of fact, I love each and every season. I can appreciate them all, but that doesn't mean I like to melt in the sweltering heat and humidity of a Kentucky summer nor does it mean I like to freeze during the cold temperatures of a Bluegrass winter. But there is magic in springtime and what it brings to our neck of the woods.

I get excited when I wake up in the mornings to hear the chirps of birds that have returned from warmer climes. I feel a stirring inside when I see the first colors of the year begin to appear on the plants and trees as they literally blossom to life. The first signs of color begin to dot the torpid landscape, reminding us that just as the Bible says in Ecclesiastes, there truly is a season for everything. The forsythia bushes' bright, yellow leaves are the first thing to bloom around our house, followed closely by the daffodils and the phlox. Watching as the color returns to the land reminds me how special this time of year is. I start looking forward to the coming months, anticipating what lies ahead. I start thinking about the tomato plants I will set out and when I need to plant them. I start daydreaming about firing up my charcoal grill and what I plan to cook on it. But there are three things that really get my blood pumping come springtime: baseball, April 17, and Easter.

As a young kid I fell in love with the game of baseball. I can remember being three or four years old sitting in the lap of my oldest brother, Artie, watching the Atlanta Braves play on TBS. We only had four channels on our TV at the time: ABC, CBS, NBC, and TBS. If you wanted to watch baseball at our house, your only option was to watch the Braves. Most people around us were Cincinnati Reds fans because they were the closest major league franchise, located just three hours from where we grew up in Jackson, Ky. I tried to like the Reds but I found myself knowing more about the Braves because that was the team I watched on a nightly basis. Before I knew it, I could no longer deny the fact I really liked the Braves a lot more than the Reds.

My favorite player for the Braves was Dale Murphy. As a matter of fact, my whole family really liked the way he played the game and the way he modeled his life and his faith for others to follow. Growing up, I can't imagine having a more perfect sports role model to look up to. Nowadays, it almost seems as if they don't make them like Murphy anymore but that's not true. Guys like Tim Tebow, R.A. Dickey, and Peyton Manning set great examples for our kids, and even though not all great role models are as prominent as these guys, you can still find them if you look for them.

Playing Little League as a kid, I tried to emulate Murphy and several other Braves and Reds players. I enjoyed playing, watching, and practicing the game. Baseball was being pumped from my heart and flowing through my veins. When Dad would get home from work, he would grab a catcher's mitt and we'd go outside so I could pitch to him. At night, when we were watching the Braves game on TV, he would pitch me a ball made of wadded-up paper, and I would practice hitting with my miniature souvenir bat I had picked up at a Reds game. Eventually, I moved my hitting to the kitchen and would toss my paper-wad balls up to myself. Mom loves to tell people about the piles of paper wads she would find behind the freezer, and it was only on a rare occasion that one of them would ask me to stop playing ball in the kitchen after they went to bed. I guess the thumping of paper balls hitting the wall interfered with their sleep. I continued to play that game in the house until I was probably in high school.

As baseball begins its annual journey out of hibernation and the flowers and trees begin to bud and blossom, it usually makes me think about April 17, 2004, the day Kristy and I exchanged vows and joined our lives together as one. I was twenty-five, she was twenty-seven, and the road we'd taken to get to this day was unimaginable. While we'd known each other since I was in fourth grade (she was in fifth), we'd been close friends for years, but neither one of us ever imagined a scenario that would lead us to this day.

We decided to have a small wedding, and I even considered eloping, but Kristy was afraid my mom wouldn't forgive her if we did. I told her it would be fine, after all Mom and Dad had eloped to Clintwood, Va., in 1967, but Kristy wasn't comfortable with the idea. Instead, we opted for a small, personal wedding, and did almost everything by ourselves. Kristy wore a stunning yellow dress, and I wore a gray suit with a purple shirt and tie. We both shed a few pounds in the three months before the wedding, and I must say we looked pretty good. The decorations were bright and colorful and instead of doing a wedding cake, we did cupcakes in five different flavors. And we did all this before there was Pinterest or Facebook!

As for the weather, which had been a major concern when we decided to do an outdoor wedding in April, it couldn't have been more perfect. We were blessed with the most beautiful day of the spring up to that point. The temperature was about 80 degrees and the sun was shining brightly. The only slight problem was the brisk wind that was wreaking havoc on our balloons. We were married on the front porch of the historic McConnell House in Wurtland, Ky., in front of about seventy family and friends. As soon as we sealed our vows with a kiss, Kristy and I danced on the front porch to Bon Jovi's "Thank You for Loving Me," a sentiment I feel daily and try to express to Kristy frequently.

But there is also someone else I need to say thanks to for the unconditional love He has given me, and all of us, and that is Jesus. Too many times in the past I've taken His love for me for granted and not appreciated or accepted it as I should. Every spring, we Christians celebrate this unconditional love of Jesus as we celebrate Easter. The Easter story serves as a reminder to us that, "For God so loved the world that He gave His only begotten Son, that whosoever believeth in Him should not perish but have everlasting life." Many of us know John 3:16 by heart because this verse encapsulates the essence of what Christ did for us and why so many people follow His teachings still today.

I love Easter and don't understand why so many Christians turn it into a somber event. I understand there is nothing joyous about the Crucifixion, but without the Crucifixion Christ wouldn't have been able to conquer death and wipe away our sins. To me, that's cause for celebration, and not just on Easter Sunday but every single day!

As you can see, I love springtime and all that comes along with it. If you ask me, it's no coincidence that within a month's time I get to celebrate the awakening of nature from its winter slumber, the return of the greatest sport ever invented, my union with the most loving, caring, and intelligent person I've ever met, and my Savior's triumphant victory over the clutches of death and sin. So, I was determined to make the spring of 2013 one of the best I've ever had.

March 16-17

I love comic books. I can't tell you the full back-story and all the story arcs a character has been through since his/her creation, but I definitely love to read comics. When I found out that the parents of one of Brayden's friends were starting a comic book convention to be hosted in Lexington in the spring of 2012, I was excited. I have longed to go to the official Comic Con in San Diego, but it would be an expensive trip and I would have a hard time missing work to get my geek on. So, having a comic convention in Lexington, a city a little more than a hundred miles from my house, I was all in. I knew it would be an easy sell to Kristy because Lexington just so happens to be one of her favorite shopping locales, but busy schedules and lack of proper planning on our part forced us to miss the inaugural Lexington Comic and Toy Convention (LCTC).

Just a matter of days after the event was held, the dates for the 2013 LCTC were announced, and I marked my calendar immediately. I was getting more and more excited about going as the months ticked away. The guest list included Margot Kidder (Lois Lane) from the Christopher Reeve *Superman* films, Peter Mayhew (Chewbacca) from the *Star Wars* movies, a slew of former Power Rangers, and several artists and actors from a wide range of comics and movie and television productions. The headliner of the convention, though, was Billy Dee Williams, or Lando Calrissian as he is better known in the *Star Wars* universe. And how could I forget all the professional and amateur (some of those I wish I could forget) cosplay performers?

I'm not one to cosplay, partially because I figured I couldn't really dress up as anyone cool and make it look right. I could've pulled off Jabba the Hutt but that would be kind of weird so I just decided to rock my *Back to the Future* T-shirt. Two of my nephews joined Kristy, our kids, and me for the event, and we had a blast. My oldest nephew, Byron, stood in line to get a Billy Dee Williams signature, and my other nephew, Travis, had his picture made with a TARDIS from *Doctor Who*. My kids ran around like crazy, grabbing anything that was free and thinking it was the most awesome thing there. The highlight of the event for me was meeting former University of Kentucky basketball player Derek Anderson, who is now an author and motivational speaker. He signed a copy of his book *Stamina*, his inspirational and personal account of how he overcame childhood adversity to become an NCAA and NBA champion as well as a USA Olympic gold medalist.

But as great as the LCTC was, and as much fun as we all had, the highlight of the weekend actually came from shopping. (The lowlight came from the weather. Sunny and 70 degrees one day; 35 degrees and a dusting of snow the next. Gotta love Kentucky.) I'd noticed over the past couple of months that I was quickly running out of clothes that fit me properly. I guess losing seventy pounds has a way of doing that. I had several items in my closet I had grown out of over the years but now they were starting to be loose and baggy. Don't get me wrong, I was excited by this but I hated the thought of having to buy new clothes, and, if I were to reach my goal of losing 150 pounds, then I might only be able to wear them for a few months before I was also replacing them. That was until I tried on a new pair of size 40 khaki pants at one of the stores and they fit comfortably. I hadn't been in a size 40 since my late-college days.

I was downright giddy after trying the pants on and having them fit perfectly. I couldn't believe I was already down eight pant sizes. Just five months before, I was wearing a size 48. At that point, I had to temper myself to keep from buying everything in the store that I thought might fit. I'd always enjoyed shopping for clothes but the last few years had been deflating. It was getting increasingly harder and harder to find clothes that fit me. Shopping for everything in the Big and Tall section of the store isn't much fun and paying a higher price for extended sizes doesn't make the ego or the wallet feel very good, either. But now I was finding clothes that fit me in the regular section of the stores.

Over the course of the next month, I went on a shopping rampage. I found some good sales on the clearance racks of a few stores. I bought sweaters in sizes L and XL thinking that I would shrink into them by the next fall. Imagine my surprise when I got them home and was able to wear them. I also bought some size 38 pants, hoping to wear them in a few months, but again was delighted to discover that the pants already fit just fine. My pant size started with a 3 for the first time in more than a decade. I was ecstatic, determined to never have a pant size that started with a 4 again.

March 31-April 7, Easter and Spring Break

It doesn't happen often but Easter and spring break came at the same time, and I was ready for a week off work. When the Lenten season began six weeks earlier, I had made a vow to better my relationship with Jesus over that time. I'm an avid reader so I decided to read nothing but Christian works from Ash Wednesday to Easter Sunday. My plan, though, wasn't only to read them but to make notes of the books I read. I typed the notes out, chapter by chapter, for each of the six books I read during that time. I saved the notes to a jump drive but also printed them out and put them in a folder to keep at home.

All the books I chose to read during this time had a profound impact on me and how I wanted to live my life. I could feel myself getting closer to Jesus and yearning to live a better life for Him, for myself, and for my family. I read two books by John Eldredge, *Desire* and *Wild at Heart*. These books opened my eyes to how I could better live my life in a way that served Jesus while getting what I most wanted out of life. I also read two books by Gary Chapman, *The Five Love Languages* and *The Five Love Languages for Kids*. These books are designed to help you love your spouse and children in the way that they best receive love, and reading them enlightened me to some things that I could do differently to be a better husband and father. I also read *Not a Fan* by Kyle Idleman and *Everybody's Normal Till You Get to*

Know Them by John Ortberg. The Idleman book is a lesson on how we as Christians can be a truly devout follower of Christ and not treat Him as if He is a famous athlete or movie star. The Ortberg book is a study on how we are dependent upon others in society and how living by the example Jesus set for us can make our community a better place.

I enjoyed reading all six books and highly recommend them. Those six weeks of reading, studying, and absorbing all that material truly made me feel much closer to Jesus. I was feeling great about where my life was headed now that I had things going in the right direction. I felt as if God was speaking to me daily as I pored over the words I was reading. It was the perfect way to get ready to celebrate the Easter season.

On Easter morn, I was glad to wake up knowing my family would be going to church to celebrate the Living Christ without persecution. What a great feeling knowing we live in a country where we can freely worship. I also received a minor blessing that day, as well. I'd planned to wear the suit I had worn on April 17, 2004, the day Kristy and I were married. When I put the suit on Easter morning, it fit better than it did nine years earlier. Kristy's mom, Sandi, had come to visit us for a few days and went to church with us. I knew if the rest of the week was going to be as good as Easter Sunday then this spring break would be hard to beat.

Of course, the rest of spring break was a bit of a disaster. We'd planned to go to visit some of Kristy's family in northern Kentucky for a few days and catch a Reds game while we were there. The baseball season was opening on April 1, and we'd ordered tickets to watch the Reds play the Angels on April 4. I was excited about the chance to see two of the game's most dominant players over the past five seasons, Albert Pujols and Josh Hamilton. But I was really stoked to see the reigning

American League Rookie of the Year, Mike Trout. I was really looking forward to the game and so was Brayden.

As it turned out, we never made it to visit Kristy's family, and we were scrambling at the last minute to get rid of our tickets to the Reds game. Misfortune befell us when Spencer began feeling bad and Kristy took him to the doctor. He was diagnosed with the flu, which caused us to cancel a sleepover Laura-Rae was supposed to have with a friend. Well, the next day, Laura-Rae began to feel poorly as well and she came down with the flu for the second time in four months. We were able to find someone to take the tickets, and I watched the game at home as I took care of two sick kids. Everyone was disappointed, but we were just thankful that we weren't traveling or at the ballgame when they became ill.

All was not lost for the week, however, as both kids were feeling better by the last Saturday of spring break so Kristy and I planned a small surprise for them. The day was beautiful and the sun was shining brightly in the cloud-sparse sky. We took the kids to Grayson Lake for a picnic. They were able to play on the playground, ride their bikes, and do a little bit of fishing. I was the only one to catch anything, but they had fun and that was all that mattered. It wasn't the spring break we had hoped for, but it also wasn't as bad as it could have been.

April 25

Spring was off to a great start and my next doctor's visit was fast approaching. I'd stopped taking my Metformin at the end of March, and my blood sugar was seemingly under control. I still checked it virtually every morning, and sometimes after eating, and it was regularly between 105 to 120. I was feeling better with each passing day, both physically and mentally, and finally realized how bad I had been feeling before changing my lifestyle. I was no longer coming home from work and just crashing on the couch or in the recliner. Most of the aches and pains in my back and knees had gone away. The negative effects of eating myself into oblivion had happened so gradually that they felt normal. After two months on the treadmill and five months of eating better, I was down to almost 300 pounds. I was still a very large man and where I had lost so much weight over a short period of time, I was getting pretty flabby in some places and decided to do something about it.

I know it sounds a little vain but since I was losing the weight, I wanted my physical appearance to be as nice as possible. I didn't want to get to my desired weight and have all this extra skin just hanging off me to where I looked like an air mattress that had been deflated. I wanted to tone my muscles with some weight training and expand my workouts beyond the treadmill. I work with several guys who are high school coaches and I used to be one myself. One thing I heard these guys talk about in doing weight training with their players was kettlebells. I'd never used one so I did some research online to see what kind of exercises you could do with one. I was astonished to see what could be done with a kettlebell.

I watched a couple of videos on YouTube and decided I had to get one of the weights so I ordered one online. I made up my own workout routine based on the videos I'd watched and did that for a couple of weeks. When we were in Lexington, Kristy actually found a video series of kettlebell workouts and bought it for me. The following week I started the videos, which concentrated on three different aspects of exercise: core strength, resistance, and cardio. I was not able to do every exercise on the videos properly but I noticed with each passing week the exercises were becoming more natural. But the best part was in a matter of two weeks, I could tell a big difference in touching my arm muscles, chest, and abs and by the time

I was scheduled to go back to the doctor, I could visibly tell a difference in those areas as well.

When April 25 arrived, I was actually looking forward to seeing Dr. Connett. I knew my body was doing much better, but I wanted her to confirm that. Since my first two visits to her office were less than enjoyable experiences, I was still looking to erase those scars from my memory, and I had a good feeling this visit would go a long way to helping me achieve that. I knew my weight was going to please her (I checked in at 292; down eighty-five pounds from October) and my blood sugar was also doing well. The one area I was really hoping to see great improvement in was the liver. My panels in January were drastically better than those from the fall but still had a ways to go to be where they needed to be.

As Dr. Connett came into the room, I was nervous. The memories of meeting her for the first time and telling me that I might have a serious heart condition that required immediate attention made a lasting impression; but upon seeing her face lit up like a Christmas tree, I knew everything was fine. She was thrilled about my weight loss and said to me, "Now that you are below 300 pounds, how about you don't go back there again, OK?" My liver function was perfect, well within normal range; sugar levels were great; cholesterol was much better, too. The most surprising thing she told me, though, came when she said "You know, I can really tell that you've been running. I can tell by looking at your heart rate. That's what a runner's heart rate looks like. You're doing great. As a matter of fact, you're doing so great that I think we can skip your next three-month appointment. Come back and see me in six months."

The only negative news was she was going to increase the dosage of my thyroid medicine to make sure it was working and to keep me from having any setbacks. Since she told me it was likely that

I would always have to take that pill upon my diagnosis, I wasn't upset by that news.

I left the building with my head held high. The sun was shining, the birds were chirping, and Brayden had a baseball game that evening. Life couldn't get any better. I knew I still had some work to do, but I felt as if I was finally on the downhill side of things. I had set a goal of losing 150 pounds in a year and I was more than halfway there. I had been eating better for six months, exercising regularly for nearly four months, and setting a great example for my kids. I was wearing sizes of clothes that I hadn't worn in more than a decade and was in the best physical condition of my life. I was ready to elevate my game and take things to a new level. I had toyed with the idea for months, but now I was ready to take a Neil Armstrong-type leap into uncharted territory. If you'd told me that one day I would be excited by making a decision like this, I would've thought you were nuts. But I'd changed many things in my life and I was looking forward to the challenge of running a 5K.

Chapter 9

Watching, Coaching, Playing

"Don't you realize that in a race everyone runs, but only one person gets the prize? So run to win!"
1 Corinthians 9:24, *New Living Translation*

"If the world were perfect, it wouldn't be."
Yogi Berra

117

From the time I was small, I was certain of one thing: I love sports. I may have subtly mentioned the fact that baseball is a passion of mine. (It's OK if you missed it. I've only referenced it a few thousand times.) But I also love football and basketball and am at least conversational in most other sports. I'm like many red-blooded American males (and females) who get wrapped up in following their favorite teams play their favorite sports. I can get crazy and forget who I am when watching a game. It happens and I'm not always proud of it, but in the years since the 1999 World Series, I have become much better at handling the failures of my favorite teams. I mostly attribute this to being a University of Kentucky football fan.

Over the years, I've had the privilege of being a fan, a participant, and even a coach. I can remember getting to watch Pete Rose play in his final season at Riverfront Stadium in Cincinnati. I got to witness Dale Murphy hit a homerun in that same ballpark. I've been to many sporting events and have even seen some sports history in person. Some of the best events I've witnessed were getting to watch Tim Tebow play during his Heisman season against the Kentucky Wildcats in Commonwealth Stadium, getting to see the Kentucky Wildcats win their first bowl game in twenty-two years in the Music City Bowl in 2006 in Nashville, being in the crowd to watch Pittsburgh make an unbelievable second-half comeback behind LeSean McCoy to beat Notre Dame in four overtimes in South Bend, and watching the Braves retire Chipper Jones's number 10 and induct him into the Braves Hall of Fame.

Not all the sporting events I've witnessed have been joyful. I was at the Daytona 500 on Feb. 18, 2001, perhaps the most historic day in NASCAR. I was at the race with Dad, Artie and Greg, Brad, and my oldest nephew, Byron. Artie, Greg, and Byron were Dale Earnhardt fans; Dad a Michael Waltrip fan; and Brad and I were Jeff Gordon fans. We were all excited about our first

Daytona experience and even had seats in Turn 4 hoping to see an exciting dash to the finish line on lap 200. Michael Waltrip won his first career race and Dale Earnhardt Jr. finished second, both drivers piloting cars fielded by Dale Earnhardt Inc., but the excitement of those feats was greatly overshadowed by Dale Earnhardt being killed in a wreck trying to block for his son and his driver to preserve their great finishes. Many say that was the day NASCAR died, and I can't say I disagree.

Over the last couple of years I've had the awesome experience of sharing sporting events with Kristy and the kids. We've attended MLB games in Cincinnati, Pittsburgh, Detroit, and Atlanta. We took Brayden to his first NCAA basketball game at Marshall University, a three-overtime thriller against Central Florida, and his first NCAA football game where we witnessed the Kentucky Wildcats end their embarrassing twenty-six-game losing streak to the University of Tennessee. We also took Brayden to Cincinnati to watch his beloved New York Giants lose to the Bengals. Even though we've made enough memories to last our lifetime, I'm looking forward to sharing more of these experiences with Laura-Rae and Spencer as they get older and we take them to watch their favorite teams in action.

As much fun as watching and participating in the events are, I can't say I always had as much fun on the coaching side of things, mostly because I was asked to help coach girls' high school volleyball, a sport I knew little about. Heck, I'd never been introduced to rally scoring until I sat on the bench for my first game. And you could forget me teaching fundamentals and techniques; I wasn't even familiar with the terminology. Combine that with the fact the head coach didn't want my help, and you had the recipe for a long season. Over the course of that season, though, I did learn a few things. One, we were a young team with only eight girls on the squad, but we were better than our 4-20 record indicated. And two, these girls desperately needed a new coach, one who was willing to put the time and energy into making them better, and who would not belittle them at every turn.

As it turned out, a new coach was hired and I became the most knowledgeable volleyball coach on a staff of two. The new coach knew nothing of the game, but he had an extensive coaching background and the passion to learn and work at it. He was able to get the girls to buy in to what he wanted to accomplish and laid the groundwork for his vision to have a successful volleyball program. All eight girls from the previous year came back, and we added four more, including a sixth-grader. We had enough girls to have a junior varsity squad, and I officially became the JV coach.

Unlike many who set out to coach, I never had that desire. I want to teach my kids how to play different sports and have fun with them in the backyard, but I've never had that desire to coach my own kids, or anyone else's for that matter. I certainly never wanted to be handed a team and be told, "Here you go. They're yours. I'll stay out of your way and let you coach them as you see fit." I felt unequipped to handle the situation. I must say, though, it was a great experience, and I found myself really enjoying what we were doing.

That same group of girls who had won only four games in 2005 was able to win nineteen the next season and make the volleyball program's first appearance in the regional tournament. I coached for three more years and was able to help lay the groundwork for a successful program. During my last season coaching, Spencer was born and I knew my time as a volleyball coach was coming to an end. I enjoyed most of my five years in that position, but I had reached my limit and it was time to turn things over to someone else. I learned to appreciate the game of volleyball, but it wasn't a passion of mine. I'd done all I could for the program and looking back I feel a great sense of pride knowing I had a hand in developing a fledgling program into a formidable regional opponent.

One thing I finally realized was that my body was much like that first volleyball team I helped coach. At the end of that first season, we were far from where we wanted to be, but within a year, that same group of girls had accomplished great things. In that same way, by the time May rolled around, I had put my body through "training camp," and less than a year after beginning this journey, it was finally ready to perform.

May 4

Making the commitment to run a 5K was a difficult decision. I knew once I signed up and paid my entry fee, there was no turning back. Once I have paid to do something, I'm going to do it unless something unforeseen happens. I had told several people I was running The Hunger Run in Raceland, I had paid for it, now I just had to do it.

I was a bundle of nerves on the morning of May 4. My stomach was turning somersaults and the butterflies would not go away. I had no idea why I was so bent out of shape about running a race but I was. It wasn't like I was pitching Game 7 of the World Series, but I have always been one to get anxious about the unknown, and running a 5K was definitely an unknown to me. I was putting pressure on myself to perform well, but I don't really know why. Finishing would be a great accomplishment no matter what my time was like.

But the nerves about the race were not the only thing that was getting to me that morning. May 4 marked the ten-year anniversary of Brad's death. In the blink of an eye, a decade had passed. So much in my life had changed in that time that I almost didn't recognize my former life. I look back at the significant events in my life up to that date and Brad had been a part of all of them. He had been much more than a cousin, a friend, or a roommate. He was as much a brother to me as Greg and Artie are and they felt the same way about him, too. Getting used to living a life without him around was surreal.

On the morning of the race, the events of ten years past were weighing on me. I couldn't help but wonder what Brad would think about me running a race. He was never one for exercise and physical activity, which is probably one of the reasons we got along so well. One thing we could both count on was that we would enable each other's bad habits.

I quickly realized battling my own emotions wouldn't be the only obstacle I had to face. The morning was beautiful, serene, and almost idyllic for my first run. The only problem was that the temperature was in the mid-fifties, and I had done all of my running indoors on a treadmill in a climate-controlled environment. To make matters worse, my allergies had decided to flare up and I had a sore throat. When you add all those things together, my apprehension level was quickly soaring off the charts.

I arrived about an hour early for the race hoping to still my nerves before getting started and hoping to establish a pre-race routine. I paced around listening to music, not really sure what I needed to be doing. The hour seemed to drag on, but with each passing minute my nerves seemed to stabilize and I was beginning to feel comfortable as the call for all racers to line up was made.

It didn't take long for me to face my first challenge after the gun was fired. The first thing I had to do was run up a hill. I'd done very little incline work on the treadmill and even though the hill was fairly short, it was pretty steep. I felt a rush of adrenaline as I dashed up the hill and was feeling pretty good about myself as the ground leveled out and I began my descent down the other side. About a quarter of a mile in, I realized my mistake. The cold air was getting to me, and my lungs were burning. I didn't pace myself up the hill and pushed too hard right out of the gate. The cool air was stinging my already sensitive throat and my lungs were on fire. I had to stop running and start walking much earlier than anticipated. As soon as I geared down, the disappointment flooded over me.

Over the next mile and a half, I bounced back and forth between running and walking. Each time I had to stop running, I would start beating myself up. I was falling apart mentally. This was something I never had to deal with on the treadmill. I knew I wasn't really competing against anyone else who was racing; I was just competing against myself. And with each step I walked it was becoming evident that I was beating myself.

Just past the halfway point of the race, I got the shot in the arm I needed to finish the race strong. I'd labored the entire race and was doubting myself. I was having thoughts that I wasn't ready to run, but then God spoke to me and reassured me that I could finish the race. The song "Can't Take the Pain" started playing on my iPod and I could feel a new strength washing over me. My legs were no longer aching, my lungs were no longer burning, and my thoughts were no longer giving in to defeat.

I was able to strongly finish the race, only stopping a few times the rest of the way. I expended the last fumes of my energy when I saw the finish line. When I crossed it, I was overcome with emotions. My time was 42:35 and I was really disappointed that it was so slow. I was hoping to get under 40:00 and felt as if I had failed. I was relieved, though, that after the way I started the race I was able to not just finish, but finish with authority. I began reflecting on how far I had come over the last seven months. I also began thinking about Brad. I was struggling to catch my breath which was compounded by the fact that I was on the verge of tears. I found a quiet place to gather myself for a couple of minutes before finding Kristy. She could tell I was disappointed, but she encouraged me, and, after a little time to reflect on things, I was proud of what I had accomplished.

June 8

I had five weeks to prepare for my next race and I was going to use that time to change my training routine. I needed to start running with more elevation on the treadmill and not hold on to the handrails of the machine as much. I knew the handrail thing would be more of a mental challenge than a physical one. I'm rather clumsy, so in my mind it was a legitimate fear that if I didn't hold on to the rails, I would more than likely get thrown off the back of the machine and through a window in the back of the living room.

During this time, my eating habits were really beginning to pay dividends. I had been off the Metformin for nearly two months, and I was able to keep my blood glucose level in the 95-110 range. Occasionally Kristy would try to get me to eat something to reward myself, and I found that I didn't really want the kinds of food I used to eat as a reward. I just didn't have an appetite for them anymore. Kristy would say, "You don't have to deprive yourself of those things. You have a handle on what you're doing." I would respond, "I'm not depriving myself. I no longer crave sweets and fatty foods. I just don't find that stuff appealing anymore." On rare occasions I would want something like that, and I would let myself have some, but I wasn't ready to fully trust myself to incorporate those things back into my regular diet, and I really was fine with that. I know there were times Kristy would get frustrated with me, but eventually she understood where I was coming from.

When June 8 finally arrived, I was excited to see how well I would do at the Run by the River. I felt amping up my routine was going to pay off and I couldn't wait to get on the course. The morning was picturesque. The temperature was much more comfortable than the first race I ran, I was feeling better, and the scenic course was serene. Virtually the entire course ran along the shores of the Ohio River in the quaint downtown area of Russell, Ky. Just being there that morning, I could feel the presence of the Lord coming over me and letting me know that He was with me that day.

I finished the race in 41:19, cutting more than a minute off my time from a month earlier. I was a little disappointed by my time but that was erased by the fact that I ran the entire race without stopping to walk one time. I hadn't anticipated being able to do that, but knowing that I had was a tremendous confidence booster for me. The only thing that really went wrong that day was I accidentally put my iPod on shuffle before the race so I had no idea what kind of time I was actually running. I was feeling so good about how I ran in the race that later that day I was inspired to write a new blog entry.

The Road Runner

It has been a few months since I have updated my health situation, and for that I am sorry. That being said, the last few months have been phenomenal. Since I last updated everyone in late March, I've lost another forty pounds, bringing my weight-loss total over the past eight months to 103, surpassing the number the doctor suggested I lose. I hope to be able to lose another forty-seven over the next four months. I'm already at my lowest weight in the past fifteen years and hope to get back to my early high school weight by the end of October.

I returned to the doctor near the end of April and received great news. The doctor was ecstatic over how well I was doing and how much weight I had lost. She officially took me off my diabetes medication because I had my blood glucose level right where it needed to be. Also, my liver functions were perfect. I can't even begin to tell you how good that made me feel to hear those things. But one of the best things she told me was that she could tell that I had been exercising because I now had the heart rate of a runner. My checkup went so well that she told me not to come back for six months instead of the normal three.

Perhaps the coolest thing that has happened over the past three months is what I was able to do on May 4 and June 8. These are the dates that I ran my first 5Ks. I was pretty nervous about the first one. It was the first time I ever ran outdoors. I had done all my running on the treadmill so I had no idea of what to expect that morning. I made a huge mistake in the first quarter mile and was not able to recover until almost halfway through the course. The run started off with a small hill and I hit it at a dead run; by the time I came down the hill on the other side and made the turn onto the main road, I was gassed. It took me probably fifteen minutes after that to find my rhythm. I finished the race with a time of 42:35 and to be honest, I was greatly disappointed. I was hoping for something in the range of 40:00. But Kristy reminded me that what I had done was still a major accomplishment. I'd done something I had never been able to do in my life and that was something to be proud of. So after sulking for a few minutes, I was able to get my mind right and appreciate my accomplishment.

I took advantage of the five weeks between the two races to change my training methods. I had intentions of doing more outdoor running but a busy schedule and nasty weather didn't allow that to happen so I had to do all my training on the treadmill again. The two things I tried to work on over this time were more elevation and not holding on to the handrails of the machine. In the end, I think modifying my strategy paid dividends. I began the race on June 8 with a much better pace and was able to run the entire race without stopping a single time to walk. Granted, most of the running was the "lineman's shuffle" but it was still running and I finished the race in 41:19. Again, I was disappointed with my results but after a minute of sulking, I received a gentle reminder from the Almighty that He was with me and that I had achieved something fantastic. To say the least it was a calming experience and one that I really needed.

As always, I know where to go to give thanks for the miracle that is happening in my life. I would be nothing without Jesus and even though there have been times I have neglected Him, I plan on giving Him the proper praise from now on. Isaiah 40:31 tells us, "but those who hope in the LORD will renew their strength. They will soar on wings like eagles; they will run and not grow weary, they will walk and not be faint." That is exactly the way I felt on Saturday, June 8. I had placed my hope in the Lord, I ran a complete race like I was on the wings of eagles, and I didn't grow weary. Until next time, I hope you all keep the faith and God bless!

Chapter 10

Travelin' Man

*"The God who made the whole world and everything
in it is the Lord of the land and the sky. He does
not live in temples built by human hands."*
Acts 17:24, *New Century Version*

"My home is in Heaven. I'm just traveling through this world."
Billy Graham

From the time I was a young boy, one thing my family always liked to do was travel. We were restricted by income and time and as my brothers got older, football; but whenever we could, we liked to go see different places and things, even if it was only a day trip. Dad always had a passion for adventure, and Mom would go wherever as long as she was with him.

The first big family trip we ever went on was in the summer of 1983 when we headed to Florida to visit Mom's Aunt Jo, who lived in Clearwater. I was just a few weeks from starting kindergarten so I don't really remember much about the trip, but the things I do remember are quite vivid. Dad had a two-tone, red and white, extended cab Ford F-150 pickup with dual fuel tanks and an extended bed that was covered in a camper shell. Back in those days there were no laws regarding child vehicular restraints, or even seatbelt laws for that matter. Or if there were, we had no knowledge of them. Dad threw a mattress down in the bed of the pickup and Artie, Greg, and I had our own little playground on the thousand mile trip to sunny Florida. Tonya sat in the back seat of the pickup and was able to stretch out and not worry about us bothering her. If we needed anything, we could open the sliding glass window of the back windshield and tell Tonya what we wanted, and she would relay the message. Imagine doing that nowadays!

Without a doubt, the highlight of the trip was going to Disney World. I'm sure I wasn't big enough to ride most of the rides, but that didn't get in the way of me having fun. The only thing that stands out clearly in my memory about that day, though, was the one thing that frightened the living daylights out of me: the Haunted Mansion. I remember waiting in line and everything was fine, then something happened, I have no recollection of what it was, but I became hysterical. Something in the Haunted Mansion terrified me, and I made no bones about being scared.

I can't even remember if I rode the ride; all I can remember is burying my face in Dad's shoulder and crying.

The other vivid memory of the trip to Florida was going to Busch Gardens. We were going across the bridge to purchase our tickets to enter the theme park when Greg suddenly lost his breakfast right there on the bridge. Thankfully, at least for Greg's sake, we hadn't paid for the tickets yet so we loaded up in the truck and went back to Aunt Jo's. She was a nurse and said she thought Greg may have swallowed too much salt water the day before when we went to a beach on the Gulf of Mexico. It's my personal belief that his swallowing all that Gulf water is why Greg could be pretty salty in his teenage years.

Over the years we took several trips to The Great Smoky Mountains, Nashville, to visit Mom's Uncle Jay in South Carolina, and various other places. But the best trip we had was to Yellowstone National Park in the summer of 1997. I had just finished my freshman year at Morehead State and was working in the warehouse of the wholesale grocery business where Dad is the bookkeeper. Tonya had four children ranging from three to nine and Artie had just moved to Michigan so neither of them was able to go. It had been a lifelong dream of Dad's to go out West and see the beautiful scenery and bountiful wildlife. He could picture himself riding on a horse following the likes of Jim Bridger or Jedediah Smith in the vast wilderness, long rifle at his side and a pouch full of hardtack and jerky. One of Dad's great passions in life is western movies and his love for those films is shared by all four of his children. To this day my favorite actor is John Wayne, and I can distinctly remember sitting in Dad's lap as a child watching John Wayne, Jimmy Stewart, Henry Fonda, Kirk Douglas, or Glenn Ford save the day in some ramshackle, lawless shanty town.

There were six of us that made the trek to Yellowstone: Mom, Dad, Greg, his wife Patty, their sixteen-month-old daughter

Kayla, and me. The trip was a 3,000-mile journey that took place over a ten-day span. Looking back, we couldn't have been in our right minds to set out on this journey. We must've evoked the spirit of the nineteenth-century settlers that loaded up their Conestogas and hit the Oregon Trail.

The farthest west I had ever been was Nashville so with each passing state and each change in scenery, I was mesmerized. The plains of Indiana, Illinois, Missouri, and Kansas were nothing but farmland. I'd never seen so much corn and soybeans. But when we reached Colorado, I really became excited. Seeing the Rocky Mountains off in the distance was like nothing I had ever seen before. Growing up in the foothills of Appalachia, I have an affinity for mountains, but I'd always read the Appalachians pale in comparison to the Rockies, and it was not until seeing them in person that I truly understood why. The majestic peaks soar out of the ground and the snow caps in the midst of summer against the azure sky were utterly breathtaking.

Wyoming was even more spectacular than Colorado. The mountains were everywhere and the land was so elevated you could see the shadows of the clouds on the ground. Purple sage and antelope stretched out across the landscape as far as the eye could see. Every other field we passed seemed to have a small herd of pronghorns grazing. All of us love seeing wildlife in its natural habitat, and Dad and Greg are avid hunters so seeing these animals graze undisturbed was fascinating for us.

When we arrived at Yellowstone National Park, I thought we were getting a glimpse of Heaven. Just looking at the beauty and natural wonders of the land and the wildlife made me feel closer to God. Seeing His wonders and appreciating them often makes me wonder how people can take the works of the Creator for granted. I have always believed the church house is not the only place to find and feel the presence of God. I can't count the times God has spoken to me as I have been observing the magnificent landscapes and natural formations He has sculpted. Romans 1:20 tells us, "For ever since the world was created, people have seen the earth and sky. Through everything God made, they can clearly see His invisible qualities—eternal power and divine nature. So they have no excuse for not knowing God." How can you argue with that?

From Yellowstone we ventured to the Black Hills of South Dakota where we went to Mount Rushmore and visited Custer State Park in Custer, S.D. It was in the middle of the state park we saw perhaps the most amazing spectacle I've ever laid eyes on. The land was nothing but rolling hill after rolling hill, which provided an excellent habitat for the American Bison. The classic country music singer Roger Miller once famously sang, "You can't roller-skate through a buffalo herd!" and he was probably right, but we were able to drive through one; albeit at a leisurely pace. There were buffalo everywhere. I'm not sure how many were in the herd, but the number was in the hundreds, and they didn't care that we were there.

We even got to see nature take its course right in the middle of the road. Growing up in an Old Regular Baptist home, copulation was not a topic that was ever brought up for discussion so when we had to stop as a bull decided to mate with a cow not five feet in front of the vehicle, Greg and I broke out into our church laugh, which we had used frequently over the years when something struck us as funny during the service. The fit of laughter looked mostly like silent convulsions, and I'm not sure why we thought we had to hide the fact that what we were witnessing was quite funny, but we never made eye contact with one another because we knew if we did, there would be no containing the outburst.

After leaving the Black Hills area and stopping at Badlands National Park, we were reaching the final leg of our trip. We had planned to stop in Lacrosse, Wis., for the last night of the trip, but we hadn't made hotel reservations. We assumed that a room would be easy to find. Well, that was before we were introduced to the Sturgis Motorcycle Rally in Sturgis, S.D. Bikers from all over the country had already started their sojourn to The Mount Rushmore State, and there wasn't a vacant room to be found off the interstate in all of Wisconsin. About 3:00 A.M., we stopped to fill the gas tank just outside of Chicago, and we asked the clerk if there was a decent hotel nearby. Now, to put this in proper perspective, you have to understand that this was the first time Dad, Greg, or I had ever been in a gas station where the clerk was locked away behind an iron cage. We don't have that in Eastern Kentucky, folks. The clerk told us, "Yeah, my buddy's mom has a place you guys can stay. I'll just give her a call and let her know you'll be coming." He gave us directions and we left the store. Once outside, we looked in the direction he told us to go and saw nothing but the pitch black night. We looked in the opposite direction and saw the lights of Chicago, and Dad said, "Boys, get in the car. We're going to Jackson." Despite our twenty-eight-hour, virtually nonstop drive from the Badlands to Jackson, Ky., that trip was one of the most enjoyable experiences of my life.

The memories of those family trips are priceless. The times I've reflected on them have made me long to be able to create those same kinds of memories for my wife and kids. I couldn't be more blessed that Kristy enjoys traveling as much as I do, and it wasn't long after we were married that she and I set out on our first great adventure together. In May 2004, we went on our honeymoon to Las Vegas. Not only was this the first time I had ever ventured on such a trip without my parents, but it was also the first, and only, time I have ever flown. We stayed at a hotel at the Port Columbus International Airport in Columbus, Ohio, the night before our flight and I was enthralled watching the commercial airliners lift off into the air as others touched down. I'd never seen anything like it. Sometimes it doesn't take much to amaze me.

I can't even begin to tell you how nervous I was the next day when the plane began to taxi down the runway. There was absolutely no turning back. For someone who is legitimately afraid of heights, the thought of zipping along 30,000 feet above the ground was more than a little unsettling. Kristy offered to take the window seat, but even though I was terrified, I was not about to miss gazing at the world beneath me.

The first hour and a half of the flight was uneventful. I was able to relax and enjoy the tapestry of the Great Midwest as it unfolded below. I had always been told that the Midwest looked like a giant patchwork quilt from an airplane and from what I could tell, that was a pretty accurate description. The fun and games ended, though, somewhere over the heartland of America when a storm rolled through and everything darkened. My view was no longer pleasant and the stewardess came over the speaker and said, "May I have your attention please. The captain has advised me that we are about to experience some turbulence. For your safety, please make sure to fasten your seatbelts." I immediately felt a sinking feeling in the pit of my stomach and any joy I had experienced up to that point was now a distant memory. The plane began bouncing and I could tell we were dropping in elevation as the wind buffeted us to and fro. I'm not sure how long the whole ordeal lasted, but it felt like hours to me. Kristy could see I was struggling so she looked at me calmly, grabbed my hand, and soothingly said, "It's OK. I've experienced much worse turbulence than this." Even though I was still uneasy, her reassuring words helped, and I was no longer on the verge of hysterics.

The rest of the flight was uneventful, and I even got excited as we flew over the Rocky Mountains. I couldn't believe how close they seemed and how breathtaking the view of the snow-covered peaks was from above. I told Kristy, "I don't know which is more impressive. Standing at the base of the Rockies looking up or soaring over them and looking down." Shortly after flying over the Rockies, we flew over the Grand Canyon. Seeing these wonders from the air was just another reminder of God's artistry and His magnificence.

By the time we had landed at McCarran International Airport in Las Vegas, I had almost forgotten about our mid-flight drama over the fruited plains. I was looking forward to a week in Vegas until Kristy said, "I'm glad we're on the ground. That was the worst turbulence I have ever been through!" I stopped walking and just looked at her. I didn't know what to say. I finally managed to get out, "Wait a minute. You told me you'd been through much worse while we were on the plane! You lied to me." She just grinned at me, dropped her head, and said, "Oops. Sorry!" I couldn't be mad at her because she'd helped calm me down and make me forget about the whole thing by the time we landed. Besides, we were in Vegas for our honeymoon.

Kristy and I fell in love with Las Vegas. Everywhere we looked, there were mountains sprouting out of the desert. The bright lights of the city were fascinating. We were amazed at how we could just walk up and down the strip and go in and out of any casino we wanted. We loved the fountain show at The Bellagio, the gondola rides at The Venetian, the mall at Caesar's Palace, and the beam of light shooting out of The Luxor. We played the penny slots, which for low rollers like us were nothing more than a glorified arcade videogame that you can win or lose a few dollars playing. One of the coolest things occurred when Kristy sat down at an old-fashioned slot machine where you actually drop a coin in a slot and pull a lever and won about $30 in quarters.

The food and entertainment were nothing short of amazing, either. We had our picture made with Penn and Teller and watched a Cirque du Soleil show. We took a bus tour to Hoover Dam and Lake Meade and laughed at our bus driver as he talked about his dam bus and all the dam tourists and the dam traffic. After we returned home from our trip, we actually looked at real estate in the Vegas area and talked about what it would be like to live there. The euphoria eventually wore off and we came back to our senses, but it was fun while it lasted. Don't get me wrong, though. As much as I loved Vegas, I can easily see how some people go astray in that town and are left broken and desperate, and I wouldn't recommend Vegas for everyone.

In the nine years Kristy and I have been married, we've also gone to Niagara Falls where we spent a night in Canada, Colonial Williamsburg, Pittsburgh, Florida several times, and several beaches. We have a map in our den that has red pins in all the locations we have traveled together and green pins in all the places we would like to travel. Over the years, I've learned to enjoy the beach and appreciate its beauty because Kristy and the kids really enjoy it, and the it is a simple vacation to take when you have three youngsters, but as someone who can get sunburned just by looking out my car windshield, the beach isn't always the most enjoyable place to go. I long for the days when the kids get a little older and we can take some trips that whet my traveling appetite.

Our 2013 summer vacation, though, had a little bit of something for everyone in the family. We spent the first part of our week in Orlando at a hotel with its own water park, and the second part of the week, I was going to watch my first Braves game in Atlanta. But what made that night even more meaningful was that the Braves were going to retire Chipper Jones's number 10 jersey on June 28, and I was going to be in the stands with my family, but not just Kristy and the kids. Dad, Greg and two of his kids, and Artie and both of his sons were coming to Atlanta for the game as well. And just when I thought nothing about that night could get any better, I was once again proven wrong, but this time in the best way imaginable.

June 22-30

As is the case with most vacations, this one came at a good time. I was in much need of a week away from daily life to recharge my battery. Even though I'm a teacher, I don't get three months off in the summertime. I teach at a juvenile detention facility, and we only get four weeks off in the summer. Three of those weeks are usually crammed with running a taxi service for the kids as I take them from one camp to another and doing various odds and ends around the house. One of the great things about being off from work, though, was that I could do my treadmill run and kettlebell workouts early and have the rest of the day to do whatever I needed to do. I tried to get as many workouts in as I could because I knew I probably wouldn't be doing any while I was on vacation.

It didn't take long after we arrived at our condo in Orlando for us to hit our fist vacation snag. The latch on the door to the condo was broken and the door wouldn't open; it wouldn't even budge. It took nearly an hour for someone from the hotel to get us into our room. The whole time we were sitting with bags of groceries strewn along the sidewalk. We were fortunate to lose no groceries in the catastrophe, but it set a bad tone for the resort. Thankfully, the rest of the stay was uneventful. The kids absolutely enjoyed the water park, and Kristy and I did too for that matter.

The only day we left the resort was to go to Legoland. We had been to Legoland the previous year and our kids loved it. Legos are a big hit at our house, and it is not unusual to see them littered across the floor of virtually every room. We were expecting this year to be even more fun than the previous year because Spencer was bigger and would be able to ride more rides. But I had a more personal reason for going back to Legoland.

When we went there in 2012, the kids asked me to get on a ride with them. I'm not a huge fan of roller coasters and carnival rides so I wasn't thrilled about getting on anything, but kids have a way of looking at you sometimes, and even though your mind is saying, "No," your mouth says, "Yes." The ride they wanted me to get on was one that lifts you straight up and then drops you down and then bounces you back up. Against my better judgment, I decided to ride with them and one of my greatest fears confronted me head-on. The girl operating the ride was struggling to get the bar fastened but nothing she tried would make it lock. After a minute or so of working with it, she leaned in to me and I could tell she was upset. She said, "Sir, the bar won't fasten with you on the ride. I'm afraid you can't ride it. I'm sorry but you'll need to get off." I don't know if she was embarrassed to tell me or if she was feeling sorry for me, but she was definitely out of sorts. Talk about a walk of shame as I had to exit the ride as everyone watched and waited. The worst part, however, was trying to explain to the kids why I wasn't allowed to ride with them. When we decided to return to Legoland, I knew I owed the kids some rides, and this time there shouldn't be anything stopping me.

Knowing that I should easily fit on the rides, though, didn't ease my mind when it came time to board the first roller coaster. I was flashing back to a year earlier and preparing myself for what it would feel like when they told me the same thing again this year. I knew my fear was irrational, but that didn't make it any less palpable. When I sat down on the coaster and the bar secured easily, I was finally able to breathe normally. I was able to ride anything I wanted to that day (or more aptly put, anything the kids wanted me to ride), but we didn't ride the bouncy ride from the year before.

The day we were leaving Orlando to head to Atlanta, we did a little shopping. I'd lost 110 pounds since October and there were very few articles of clothing that had survived the mass cleanout of my wardrobe. I was now going through clothes so quickly that I only had the opportunity to wear some things once or twice before they were too large for me. I'd never been in that situation before. On one hand, I was thrilled, but on the other, I hated to keep spending money on clothes. I'd made the decision early on to try to buy everything off the clearance racks and to try to anticipate sizes and buy ahead when possible, but even that was a bit of a crapshoot.

Each time I dropped a size in pants, I was speechless. Imagine my surprise, however, when we were shopping in Orlando and I tried on a pair of size 36 pants only to discover that the pants fit perfectly. It was difficult to fathom that when I started on this journey I was wearing size 48 pants. I had to control my excitement and not buy every pair of size 36 pants on every rack in every store we entered.

When Kristy and I first started dating, I really enjoyed going shopping with her; but over the years, shopping had become a frustrating experience. Many of the stores I liked to shop at didn't have clothes my size, and the ones that did often had a limited selection of clothing for my taste. It was a nice feeling to actually enjoy going shopping again.

As much fun as shopping was, I couldn't wait to get to Atlanta because that was where the highlight of the trip was waiting for me. Chipper Jones was my second-favorite Braves player of all-time. He was the same age as Artie so it was not like Chipper was a childhood hero of mine, but I had watched his entire career, which spanned half my life, and he had become Brayden's favorite player.

We stayed at a hotel across the street from Turner Field so we could go over to the field early and explore. We took pictures of all the retired numbers and the statues outside the stadium as we waited for the rest of our crew to show up. As the gates to the stadium were nearly open, Dad, Greg, Artie, and children arrived. Artie and I hadn't seen each other since Christmas and my appearance had changed quite a bit over that six-month period. When he came up to me he said, "I'm not sure I would have recognized you if I wasn't with Dad and Greg." I was actually taken aback by his comment. I was wearing a baseball cap and sunglasses but I wasn't expecting my own brother to not recognize me. Then he said, "It was the beard that was throwing me off." I couldn't help but laugh because if you had seen the sorry excuse for a goatee I was sporting you would have known that wouldn't have made me unrecognizable.

Once we entered the stadium, one of the most unexpected thrills of my life occurred when Greg discovered that Dale Murphy, my all-time favorite Braves player, was signing autographs at a designated area of the stadium. I knew many former Braves would be there because the Braves franchise usually does their homecoming when they are retiring a number. Never in my wildest dreams, though, did I imagine Dale Murphy was going to be one of those former players on hand to sign. After standing in line for nearly an hour, a wait that was well worth it, I finally got to meet and shake hands with my childhood hero as he signed a baseball for me.

Even though getting to meet Murphy was the highlight of the night (and the entire trip for that matter), the night only got better. The retirement ceremony for Chipper Jones's number 10 was a classy event, punctuated with a 3-0 Braves win over the

Arizona Diamondbacks. As we left the stadium to go to Artie's house in Sweetwater, Tenn., I was on Cloud Nine. I had just experienced the greatest sporting event of my life. Little did I know that I could only make that claim for three months.

Chapter 11

Walking in Faith

*"For by grace you have been saved through faith. And
this is not your own doing; it is the gift of God."*
Ephesians 2:8, *English Standard Version*

*"If fear is cultivated, it will become stronger. If
faith is cultivated, it will achieve mastery."*
John Paul Jones

One of the greatest aspects of my life growing up was going to church. I'm sure there were times I took it for granted that I was being raised in a family that valued the tenets of the Christian faith, and there was a time I turned away from those beliefs, but deep down in my soul I always knew I was being raised right, and when I was raising a family of my own, I wanted to be able to raise them the same way.

The pastor at the church I attended growing up was my pappaw, Bess Gross. Pappaw was certainly a self-made man. He dropped out of school in middle school, but his lack of formal education did not prevent him from raising a happy family and spreading the Gospel. He didn't have a high school diploma or a degree from seminary, but I would challenge anybody to find someone more knowledgeable about Scripture. He was the perfect role model of what a father and husband should be and he passed that along to my father as well. I've always said if I could be half the husband and father they have been, then I would be just fine.

The church Pappaw pastored was an old country church that was mostly attended by the Gross family and some of their in-laws. Pappaw and Mammaw raised seven children, and all seven attended the Old Regular Baptist church with their families. It was great getting to worship and fellowship with our aunts, uncles, and cousins, knowing that they were also our brothers and sisters in Christ. I wouldn't trade that kind of upbringing for anything in the world.

After the fourth Sunday service of the month, the whole family would gather at Pappaw's and Mammaw's house for a huge potluck meal. It was always exciting to ask our cousins what dishes our aunts had made, and then we would sit through the service and salivate thinking about the forthcoming meal. As a child, I had no idea what kind of preparation it took for these women to make these dishes while getting themselves and their children ready for church. And this was long before the rampant use of Crock-Pots and slow cookers, too.

But eating was not the only skill I honed after church on Sundays. In the spring and summer, I would go down to the creek bank that flowed past the church house with my brothers and cousins and we would play baseball, only we didn't have a bat or a ball. In lieu of those necessary items, we would improvise with sturdy sticks or tree branches that had washed up on the bank or fallen from the nearby trees for bats and we would pitch gravels instead of a ball. Using the thin-barreled makeshift bats to hit the tiny rocks no doubt improved our hand-eye coordination and helped all of us with our baseball skills. There were many times our parents would scold us and tell us we were going to hurt someone with the gravels, but their threats in this instance were mostly idle, and we were undeterred in our pursuit of playing baseball.

As great as food and baseball were, I didn't realize until I was much older those two things weren't the most important thing happening to me on the Sundays of my youth. I was having the foundation of a better life laid within my heart. Listening to Pappaw and Uncle Lige preach and sitting in Sunday school classes taught by Aunt Lois, Mom, and Dad taught me valuable lessons about living a Christian life. Even though I'd always identified myself as a Christian and believed it in my heart, I didn't make my public confession and accept Christ formally until May 3, 1997, and I was baptized eight days later at the boat dock of Panbowl Lake in Jackson. As I was coming up out of the water, I could feel the Holy Spirit wash over me, and the sky above never looked as heavenly as it did at that moment.

Little did I know that after being baptized and formally becoming a Christian, the hard part was only beginning. For the next seven years of my life, I was farther from Christ than I'd ever been. It wasn't until Kristy and I were married that I was able to regain my footing and begin walking in faith again. There have been many times over the past nine years that I have strayed, but I know where to look when I need to get back on the path. Now more than ever it is important for me to follow the path of Christ and set the example for Brayden, Laura-Rae, and Spencer that Dad, Mom, Pappaw, Mammaw, and others set for me when I was growing up. After all, the Bible tells us in Proverbs 22:6, "Train up a child in the way he should go; even when he is old he will not depart from it." I know that has been true in my case, and I hope and pray I'm doing what's necessary to train my children the same way I was trained. On the day that our country was celebrating its 237th birthday, I received some confirmation that I was doing something right along those lines.

July 4-August 9

After returning from vacation, my battery was recharged and I was feeling good about what I had accomplished. I had almost three months until I returned to the doctor for my year follow-up and I didn't have any more 5Ks planned until the middle of August. I hadn't run on the treadmill for nearly ten days while we were on our trip, but the layoff didn't affect me. In fact, in many ways I felt stronger on the treadmill and pushed myself harder.

Even though I managed to not gain any weight on vacation, a fact that absolutely thrilled me, I did notice that after returning from Florida the weight was not coming off quite as easily. I wasn't doing anything different but I had hit a wall. I figured hitting two walls in nine months was probably not too bad so I didn't panic.

Overall I was feeling pretty great about the way things were going. I was now wearing a size 36 in pants and actually bought a couple pair of shorts in a size 34 when we were on vacation. I was buying a size XL in shirts and even bought some undershirts in a large. I hadn't been in those sizes since starting college seventeen years earlier. But even as great as I was feeling about how far I had come in transforming my body and improving my health, the greatest feeling came on July 4.

Every year during the summer we send the kids to various camps in the area to keep them busy doing things and not just sitting around finding ways to get bored. Most of the camps we send them to are educational, but we had the opportunity to send Brayden to Winshape Camp at a nearby church. Winshape is a foundation that was started by Truett Cathy, founder of Chick-fil-A, with the purpose of strengthening families and bringing them closer to God. Each year they send camp counselors to various church destinations across the nation in hopes of bringing young people Christ's message. We were thrilled to be able to send Brayden to the camp, and he was excited because he knew several of his friends were also attending.

Each day when he came home from camp, Brayden would tell us about the exciting things he had participated in and would talk about the Bible lesson for that day. On the fourth day of camp he came home and made an announcement to Kristy and me. "Mommy? Daddy? I gave my heart to the Lord today. I want to get baptized." Kristy and I were taken aback at first, but we couldn't have been more proud of him. We sat down with him later and talked to him about the decision he made and tried to get a feel about whether he understood what his decision meant. After talking with him, we knew he understood what impact his decision would have on his life. Ten days later, Brayden was baptized in my parents' pool; Dad did the ceremony and I stood in the pool with them to assist. Just as when I was baptized, I could feel the presence of the Almighty shining down on us.

Over the next few weeks, I continued to work hard preparing for my next 5K. It was going to be a race like none of the others that I had run, but I was confident it would help me get prepared for the Monster Mash and Dash in October, since both races would be at night. I was eager to see how I would fare after working all day and running at the end of the day instead of at the beginning. My goal was to finish below 40:00 and to run the entire race without stopping. I was able to accomplish both goals, but the real story wasn't what I'd achieved but how I achieved it. I was so amazed and awestruck by what happened to me during that race that it took me a week to collect my thoughts before putting my experience into words. I felt as if I had no choice but to share with everyone the small miracle that happened to me that night.

Miracles Come in All Sizes

I have always believed in God. I've often felt the presence of God in my life. Sometimes it is easier to recognize God's presence than others. Obviously, on the days my children were born, I felt God's presence in my life intensely. I could also feel the same unmistakable presence as I was coming up out of the water in Panbowl Lake on the day I was baptized. Other times, that presence has been more subtle but no less reassuring. But last Friday night, I had an experience I had never had before. Not only did I feel the presence of God, I felt the physical touch of God. Some of you may dismiss what I'm about to tell you and that's fine; you have the right to do so. But I know what I felt and the only way I can explain it is the Holy Spirit lifted me up and kept me running.

Last Friday evening, I ran my third 5K. It didn't start until 9:30 at night so I was curious to see how my body would respond to running so late after working all day then spending several hours at home. Normally, I do my running on the treadmill as soon as I get home from work. If I run on Saturdays, I usually run as soon as I get up in the morning. Knowing my routine, I was pretty sure this race was going to present a challenge for me, and I wasn't wrong.

I started the race at a good pace and was feeling really good about the way things were going. More people had signed up for the race than I had anticipated, but I knew I was not competing against them because I had my own goals already established. As usual, I didn't want to finish last and I wanted to be able to run the entire race without walking. The biggest goal for me, though, was to finish the race in less than 40:00, which meant I would need to cut off nearly 1:20 from my previous 5K in June.

The course was three laps and after running the first lap, I was feeling really good. I glanced at the timer at the start/finish line and could tell that my time was under 13:00 for the first lap. The second lap was becoming more of a struggle and I could feel my legs starting to get tired about halfway through the lap. I muttered a prayer asking God to keep me going as long as He possibly could. I really didn't want to have to walk but my legs were beginning to feel a little rubbery. The clock was just under 26:00 as I started my third lap.

My struggle intensified, and I knew it would take a miracle to complete the race without walking. And that is exactly what happened. About one-third of the way through the final lap, my legs sent a message to my brain that they were done. Finished. Not able to run another step. I could feel my legs going from a trot to a walk and there was nothing I could do about it. But God could. I was trying to prepare myself to mentally finish the rest of the race despite taking a few seconds to walk when I felt something wash over the lower part of my body. For three steps, it was as if I were walking on air. I literally did not feel the ground for three steps. I wasn't numb because I could feel a presence touching my legs and then I started to run a little faster. I was renewed and was able to finish the race strongly with a time of 39:23. If I had slowed down and walked like my body had wanted, I wouldn't have reached my goal of finishing in less than 40:00.

Now, by calling this a miracle I'm in no way comparing it to Jesus turning the water into wine or to feeding the masses with just a few fish and a few loaves of bread. I'm certainly not comparing it to healing the blind, raising people from the dead, casting out demons, or conquering death and washing away our sins. But in my opinion, it definitely qualified as a minor miracle. Matthew 21:22 tells us, "And whatever you ask in prayer, you will receive, if you have faith." I prayed and I received. Acts 1:8 says, "But you will receive power when the Holy Spirit comes upon you, and you will be my witness . . . to the end of the world." I can attest to feeling the power so now I am fulfilling my obligation to witness.

As I said earlier, I had felt the presence of the Holy Spirit many times, but actually feeling the touch of the Spirit is indescribable. I know it was just a little 5K in Ashland, Ky., on a Friday night, but God saw fit to let me know He was with me, and He has been with me since I started this journey ten months ago. In October, I was facing the most daunting challenge I had ever been faced with. It was literally a matter of life and death. I chose to fight for life and God has been with me every step of the way and for that I am eternally thankful. I could try to find the proper words to express my gratitude but Psalm 28:7 sums it up best: "The Lord is my strength and my shield; in Him my heart trusts, and I am helped; my heart exults, and with my song I give thanks to Him." Until next time, keep the faith good people. I know I certainly will.

Chapter 12

Finishing Strong

"For the Lord your God is the one who goes with you to fight for you against your enemies to give you victory."
Deuteronomy 20:4, *New International Version*

"We are never defeated unless we give up on God."
Ronald Reagan

Summer was coming to a close and the autumn air had already arrived in Eastern Kentucky. I was now entering the homestretch. I realized with a little more than a month to go before going back to the doctor I wasn't going to meet my weight-loss goal of 150 pounds, but I figured even if I only reached 90 percent of the goal, I would be doing fantastic. I had stepped up my work on the treadmill and ran another race in early September on the same scenic Ohio River course that I ran back in June, and I finished with a time even better than I had hoped for. My only real goals were to finish with a better time than I did in August and to run the entire race. I was completely floored when I finished the race more than three minutes quicker than my previous time. I finished in 36:03, and my first thought was actually disappointment that I couldn't finish four seconds faster.

The following week I received an unexpected health scare. Due to my fair complexion, freckled skin, and propensity to get sunburned on the cloudiest of days, I pay a visit to a dermatologist for an annual checkup. The first year I visited the dermatologist, everything checked out fine so I expected nothing to change. If you haven't figured it out by now, I'm not very good at diagnosing my own medical predicaments. The doctor discovered a mole in the center of my lower back had started to look strange in comparison to the previous year. She removed the mole and sent it off to be evaluated. A week later I received a phone call from a nurse at the dermatologist's office. "Mr. Gross? We have the results of your biopsy. The tests show there were some pre-cancerous cells. The doctor wants you to come back in so she can remove a larger area." My first thought was, *I really need to stop taking these calls at work.* She scheduled me to come back to the office in the middle of October to undergo the precautionary procedure.

I was astonished by the results and wasn't really sure how to feel about what I had just heard. I called Kristy immediately and told her about my latest medical development. I couldn't help but think about Brad. The nurse had made the procedure seem like no big deal, but the term "pre-cancerous" put me on edge. I knew I was at a higher risk of skin cancer than others, and I had firsthand experience in dealing with the devastation a disease like melanoma brings with it. Knowing that my mind has a tendency to run wild with worst-case scenarios, I harkened back to what my gut told me to do when I visited Dr. Connett for the first time and failed my EKG. I said a quick prayer and turned it over to God because there was nothing I could do about it. Besides, I had plenty of fun things planned that would keep my mind occupied over the next month, and I didn't want to ruin them by being worried about something that was beyond my control.

October 4-5

One night early in September, Kristy surprised me with some news. Out of the blue, she asked me, "What do you want to do over your fall break next month?"

I thought about it for a second and came up with nothing. "Uh, I don't know. Hadn't really thought about it. Why? Do you have something in mind?"

"I thought we might go to Atlanta for a few days. Thought you might want to watch the Braves in the playoffs." Unbeknownst to me she'd been paying attention to when the playoff tickets went on sale and had already ordered two. I was shocked. I had always wanted to watch the Braves play in the playoffs, but figured it was only wishful thinking.

Perhaps the more amazing thing, though, was that for the first time, Kristy and I were going on a trip without the kids. I realize that for many families it's common to take little getaways without children, but the logistics to make that happen had always been problematic for us. Needless to say, though, I was stoked about making the trip. I thought going to the game in June and meeting Dale Murphy and seeing Chipper Jones's number get retired couldn't be topped, but obviously it could be.

The Braves had sustained some injuries causing them to limp, both literally and figuratively, into the playoffs to do battle with the hottest team in baseball since mid-June, the Los Angeles Dodgers. Atlanta lost the first game of the series, and I was desperately hoping they would pull off a victory in the second game. Kristy and I arrived at the stadium early and entered as soon as the gates opened, three hours before the first pitch. We headed immediately to the Braves dugout to get the best possible view of the field. The Braves players were taking the field for their pregame routine. I stood there in awe as I watched Brian McCann, Freddie Freeman, Craig Kimbrel, Evan Gattis, the Upton brothers, and the rest of the team warm up. I felt as if I was in my own personal Field of Dreams as I watched these grown men preparing to play a child's game. We stood and watched for more than an hour as the Braves players played long toss, took infield, shagged flies, and took batting practice.

When the Braves finished their pregame routine, we made our way over to our seats down the third baseline to watch the Dodgers warm up. While watching them go through their routine wasn't as exciting as watching the Braves, it was still pretty awesome to be up close watching Major League ballplayers doing their thing. The highlight of watching the Dodgers on the field, though, was the pleasant surprise of getting to see NBA Hall of Famer and co-owner of the Dodgers franchise Magic Johnson as he was doing interviews with the media in front of the visitors' dugout.

The game itself was electric and my wish was granted as the Braves managed to get their only victory of the series, winning 4-3. Braves starting pitcher Mike Minor threw like an ace, and Craig Kimbrel came on in the eighth and closed the door. The rest of the series belonged to the Dodgers as they had their way with Atlanta, but I was thankful the Braves were able to win the game Kristy and I attended.

The next day, Kristy and I casually kicked around Atlanta. We went to the Margaret Mitchell House where the famous author wrote the great Civil War classic, *Gone with the Wind*. Kristy is a huge fan of *Gone with the Wind* so she was excited about getting to tour the museum. From there, we went to the Coca-Cola Museum, rode a giant Ferris wheel, and then checked out the lobby of CNN Center. All in all, it was a pretty great trip for the both of us.

October 12-16

When I made a commitment to get myself in better shape, I decided the Monster Mash and Dash was going to be my Super Bowl. There is nothing special about the race, though, from the standpoint of it being historically significant or anything like that. The reason it resonates with me is because it's organized by the juvenile detention center where I teach and raises money for three different charities, including the American Cancer Society. The event, always held at Ashland's Central Park, was entering its third year and has grown in popularity. It has practically become a mini-festival to promote health while also celebrating Halloween. For no other reason than I had personal ties to the event, I made it the focal point of my young racing career.

Truth be told, though, I had actually tried to run the Monster Mash and Dash during the inaugural year, but that was nothing short of a disaster. To start with, I was terribly out of shape. In my warped mind I figured I could run/walk the whole race and not embarrass myself. I did zero training for the event and thought showing up in a Dri-FIT shirt and windbreaker pants would be my secret weapon. To make matters worse, I signed up for the stroller division thinking I could push a double stroller around the park for three miles and maybe even get a medal. Pretty sound logic, don't you think?

But there was one thing I wasn't counting on: a nasty stomach virus. Just before going to the event, I was bent over a toilet emptying my guts. My head was swimming and I was woozy, but I figured I would soldier on and perform like Michael Jordan when he had the flu. Just before the race started, another complication arose. Brayden began feeling ill and decided to get into the stroller. I had planned on pushing Laura-Rae and Spencer around the park but substituting Brayden for Laura-Rae added an additional thirty pounds to the buggy.

It didn't take me long to realize I had bitten off more than I could chew, and in those days I could chew a lot. It took approximately 3.5 seconds for me to establish a firm foothold on last place and by the time I turned the first corner, I had almost lost sight of the other competitors. Somehow, I managed to complete the first lap of the two-and-a-half-lap race and called it quits. I blamed my poor performance on the stomach bug, and it certainly was a factor, but the real reason was I had underestimated the degree of difficulty of the race and overestimated my own abilities and physical condition.

In some ways I think I was looking for redemption because several of my co-workers witnessed the colossal failure of that first year, but they were all too kind to point out the obvious. Other than Kristy and the kids, no one has witnessed my transformation as closely as my co-workers. I can't say enough great things about the support, compliments, and interest they have taken during this process, and I can't imagine working with a greater group of people than I currently work with. By redemption, though, I'm not talking about trying to prove something to them. I just wanted to show them the fruits of my labor and let them see how much their support meant to me.

When the night of the race arrived, the air had a slight chill to it, but I was confident once I found my rhythm it wouldn't affect me. I'd learned a lot about running and pacing myself since May and that chilly morning when I ran my first 5K. There were more than 300 people participating in the race and, as always, I didn't want to finish last, which at this point was an irrational concern. I finished the race in 37:20, not a career best, but still a nice finish. The only problem I encountered was the crowded sidewalk. Where I had completely dogged it two years earlier and had plenty of room in the back of the pack, I hadn't anticipated the course to be so crowded and tight. Other than that, I was overjoyed with the way the night had gone.

It had been a year and two days since my initial doctor's visit and so much had changed in my life. If I'd continued along the path I had been on 367 days earlier, it's quite probable that I would've weighed more than 400 pounds, been in failing health, or even quite possibly dead. To say the least, that's a rather sobering thought. I'd taken action when action was needed, without delay and without complaint. I changed my life for the better. I was setting a shining example for my children. I was much healthier physically, mentally, and even spiritually than I had ever been in my life. Looking back, I almost couldn't recognize myself and when I say that, I'm not only referring to my physical appearance. I was like the old house in *It's a Wonderful Life* that Mary Bailey loved and dreamed of living in but others saw as a dilapidated eyesore. Eventually, it became a fine house for George and Mary to raise their family in; all it needed was a chance and some elbow grease for that potential to be fulfilled. That is how my body and my life were. I was rundown on the outside and the inside. I was in need of repair and what seemed like the worst news of my life turned out to be perhaps the greatest blessing in disguise I could ever have imagined. I'd been given a second chance at life, and I grabbed it with both hands and haven't let go. I was presented with a problem that wasn't too big for God, nothing is, and one that He could help me control. Now I just had to let Him take the reins on the problem that was beyond my control.

Four days after the race, I went back to the dermatologist to get a larger hole cut in my back to hopefully remove the rest of the ugly cells from the area where I formerly had a nasty mole. Strangely enough, I was at ease. I turned it over to a higher power a month earlier, and I was letting Him do His work and trying to stay out of His way. As far as procedures go, this one was unobtrusive and not as painful as I expected. The dermatologist assured me the procedure was routine and even told me, "Hey, I've had this procedure several times. It really isn't a big deal." A few weeks later I received news that the biopsy was clear and all looked good. Even though I hadn't worried myself to death about it, I couldn't help but feel the overwhelming sense of relief upon hearing that news. With that out of the way, I just had one more doctor's visit left.

October 25

A year and two weeks had passed since the initial visit that allowed me to retake control of my life. I had a great feeling about the news I was going to receive from Dr. Connett, and for once, my no-big-deal attitude was correct. Dr. Connett was astounded by the change I had undergone in a year's time. She showered me with compliments the whole time. "I had a feeling when I had to tell you that terrible news last year that you were a determined person. I knew you could do this." I just smiled at her but didn't tell her when I left that day I couldn't have been more unsure about my resolve.

Let me just take a moment to tell everyone how thankful I am for Dr. Connett. When I first met her in October 2012, she had to tell me some really bad things about myself and my health, and the one thing that stuck with me was that she felt sorry for me. I could see it in her eyes and in her demeanor. What I didn't figure out until later visits was I had misread her. She didn't feel sorry for me; she cared about me and what I was doing to myself. She wanted to see me turn my life around so I could be there for my family for years to come. It wasn't pity I saw on her face; it was compassion. I had never seen that from any of the doctors I had visited in the past. Realizing that she hadn't given up on me and she was actually in my corner the whole time made me understand she had delivered this news to too many people who hadn't taken heed of her words.

The whole time she was talking to me, a broad smile never left her face and the sparkle never left her eyes. I could genuinely sense how proud of me she truly was. "You are living proof that weight-loss can happen naturally without surgery." Although I had never actually voiced that sentiment myself, I, too, was proud of that fact. When I first started this journey I told myself I wanted to avoid surgery at all costs. I'm not against the surgical weight-loss procedures; I know several who have had great success after having the surgery. But on the flipside, I also know of several people who experienced the nightmarish side of the procedure. In my mind, though, being able to lose weight by eating healthier, exercising, and changing my lifestyle would be the equivalent of beating a videogame without using a strategy guide or cheat codes.

As crippling as the sense of dread and the unknown were a year earlier when I left her office, this time I felt as if my shackles had been loosed and my spirit had been set free. Before leaving, I had a favor to ask of the good doctor. "Dr. Connett? Can you do something for me? I'm writing a book about my experience. Can you write a letter for me to include?" She replied, "Absolutely. I'd be more than happy to do that for you." Here is what she wrote:

> As a family practice physician, I have the unique opportunity to meet people of all walks of life and treat a wide variety of illnesses. I am inspired every day by the battles of my patients and Brian Gross is no exception. I first met Brian in October 2012 for a basic physical. He reported being relatively healthy despite his 377-pound weight on his 72-inch frame at 34 years old. We took basic blood work and found he was anything but healthy. At only 34 years old, Brian was a new Type II diabetic with a fatty liver, elevated cholesterol, low testosterone, and hypothyroidism. I asked Brian to come to the office to discuss the findings. With his wife at his side, we went through the findings one by one. He sat quietly engaged. I spoke candidly about his weight and the effects on his health. He told me he would try to lose the weight and I believed in him. We used medicines initially with the understanding these would be temporary if he lost the weight.
>
> I saw Brian every three months to reassess his values. On January 18, 2013, he weighed 328. I knew I had a fighter. He was determined to change. He continued to lose and a year later, October 25, 2013, he weighed 243 pounds. Brian lost more than 130 pounds in a year.

This is not a story of surgical weight-loss nor gimmicky diets. Brian changed his life with portion control and exercise. I nearly cried with happiness to report all values were normal one year later with only a thyroid medicine.

His motivation and determination have inspired me personally and professionally. He is proof it can be done.

Carrie Connett, D.O.

Reading that letter for the first time nearly brought tears to my eyes. At no point in my life had I ever imagined my name would be associated with the word inspirational. Even when I felt the calling to write about my experiences, being an inspiration to others never crossed my mind. At first, I was only motivated by fear to be healthier for myself, my wife, and my children. Over the course of the past year, I've been motivated to be a shining light, an instrument of Jesus Christ, an inspirational tale that the seemingly impossible can be achieved. After all, the Bible tells us in 2 Timothy 1:7, "For God gave us a spirit not of fear but of power and love and self-control." Had I not turned my fear over to God in the beginning of this trial, I never would have discovered the power, the love, and the self-control to slay my own personal dragon. I still have a long way to go, but the hardest part of the battle has already been fought and won. What easily could've been the beginning of the end for me became the end of one phase in my life and the beginning of a much brighter one.

Afterword

"For I can do everything through Christ, who gives me strength."
Philippians 4:13, *New Living Translation*

*"In order to succeed, your desire for success should
be greater than your fear of failure."*
Bill Cosby

Fifteen months have now passed. Five seasons have come and gone. Along with those months and seasons, 150 pounds have also been shed. I had no idea what my life would be like fifteen months after being presented with this daunting challenge. At times it hasn't been easy, but it hasn't been as difficult as I had feared either. The hardest part, as with anything, was getting started. In my case, I suppose the beginning was a little easier due to the fact I was afraid to eat. Food, something meant to sustain life, had become something that was taking mine. Fear is indeed a great motivator, but at some point fear has to be conquered. (Remember what Yoda said? "Fear is the path to the dark side. Fear leads to anger. Anger leads to hate. Hate leads to suffering.") Once I gave up my fear, my life changed for the better, and I knew I would be successful in restoring my temple.

It can be done and the process doesn't have to make your life miserable. Make no mistake, I love food. But the love of food can be as damaging as the love of money. Do we need food? Of course. Do we need money? Absolutely. Do we need to let them control our lives and motivate our desires? Absolutely not! When we take something that is meant to be good and make it more than what it is, we create problems. In essence, when we replace God with food, money, sex, or anything else, we are setting ourselves up for a massive failure. And the more we let that stuff control us, the harder the fall is. It's only when we turn to God to deliver us from the clutches of these things that we can truly make progress. Remember, all of these things are good, but they have their place in life.

If you are reading this and you have battled weight problems and subsequent health issues, I want you to know there is hope for you. I've been there and I know how it feels to be consumed by something intended to be good and enjoyable. If eating food was an unpleasant task, then no one would ever have a problem with being overweight. But it is enjoyable and like so many things that we allow to control us, we are susceptible to the ills of excess. But no matter how dark things may seem, know there is light at the end of the tunnel. Let me share a few tips on how I have turned my life around.

1. **Supplication and Relinquishing Control**: For some, this may be the hardest step. It wasn't difficult for me to turn to Jesus in my time of need and let go of the fear and worry. I needed to put God back in first place and tell the food to take a backseat. I was raised in church and have always been a believer. Praying is not unnatural for me, but I realize that for many it's a foreign concept. All I can say is if you are uncomfortable and don't know where to start, just put it out there. Rip the bandage off quickly, so to speak. When praying to an omniscient power, remember He already knows so you might as well be frank about it. Or just remember Philippians 4:6. "Do not be anxious about anything, but in everything by prayer and supplication with thanksgiving let your requests be made known to God." It really is as simple as that. Let go and let God. You'll be glad you did.

2. **Control Your Food. Don't Let It Control You.** Many of us have this one backwards. I know I did for the longest time. Food is meant to strengthen us, to keep us going. It wasn't designed to harm us. We need it to live; not to help us die. Anyone who loves food knows this is a difficult concept, but it must be grasped. And do me, and yourself, a favor and get rid of the excuses. I know them all. I realize some healthy food doesn't taste as good as its unhealthy counterpart, but you need to remember which one you need, not which one you want. Like most great things, unhealthy foods are great in moderation, but many times we don't stop at moderate. We floor the pedal and head for excess, and

that's what gets us in trouble. Before all this, I never ate cooked cabbage, sweet potatoes, Brussels sprouts, or yogurt. But I quit looking at them as the enemy and instead embraced them as a friend. I knew they would treat me better, and at the end of the day isn't that what we should want? We all know the Golden Rule from Matthew 7:12 that goes as follows: "Do to others what you want them to do to you." Well, the Golden Rule of Food needs to be, "Eat the food that treats you the way you would like people to treat you." Once you grasp this, eating can still be enjoyable and much more beneficial.

3. **Run, Forrest, Run.** You need to get physically active. There are no ifs, ands, or buts about it. Doctors tell us we need exercise and we know they're right, but many of us had just rather not. (Again, this is an excuse-free zone. I don't want to hear them because I've used them all.) Just as with healthy food, you must stop thinking of exercise as the enemy. You can choose whatever type of physical exercise you're most comfortable with, but my preferred method is running and for me to say that is a testament in its own right. I used to hate running and could never understand people who said they loved it. I thought they were nuts. Now, I'm one of those nuts. We bought a treadmill and used it as a space filler in the back of the living room for about six months. Now, it's the most used appliance in the house. When I started running in January 2013, I set some goals but I didn't really know what I was capable of doing. My distance goal for the year was to walk/run 365 miles, an average of one mile per day. I finished 2013 by walking/running 505 miles, exceeding my initial goal by 38.4 percent. I also set a goal to burn 35,000 calories. I smashed that one by burning more than 76,000. Some days I felt like Forrest Gump. I would start running on the treadmill and I would just keep running and running.

4. **Make It Yourself**. Make your own food. Cooking is fun and by doing it yourself, you know exactly what you are putting in your meals. Eating healthy doesn't have to be a chore. One of the best things over the past year has been discovering new recipes and making them for the family. I do about 80 percent of the cooking at our house which means I control what my family is putting in their bodies, at least when we eat at home. I can honestly say that there have been only a few times over the course of this journey that I've been hungry. I fix filling, healthy meals and eat till I am full, not stuffed. There are several websites, cookbooks, magazines, and TV shows that can assist you. If you are a novice cook, especially a male, don't be intimidated. Cooking isn't that difficult. In fact, all the men in the Gross family are really good cooks, and they all do their share of fixing meals. We learned from Mom and she certainly knows her way around the kitchen. By making your own meals at home, you can save money, eat healthier as a family, and enjoy the experience of trying new things.

5. **Embrace the Lifestyle**. Don't look at what you are doing as a diet. You need to realize you're undergoing a lifestyle change. Diets come and go, but a true change in your lifestyle means you're doing what is best for you for the rest of your life. Accept that fact and embrace it. It may take some longer than others, but if you don't come around to that way of thinking, your success will be hard to sustain. You must approach the change with a positive attitude or you will positively fail. Once you accept that what you are doing will improve your living condition, and hopefully assist in prolonging your life, it makes things easier. You must stay determined and committed to make it work, but if I can do it, anybody can. And I'm not just saying that, either.

6. **Be Patient**. Since it is a lifestyle change, you need to understand it's OK if the results come slowly at times. Life is meant to be a marathon, not a sprint. If you are only losing a pound a week, then over the course of a year you will lose more than fifty pounds. Over two years, you'll surpass the century mark. Results will vary for each person. One of the worst things you can do is compare your progress to someone else's. Everybody's body is different and will respond in different ways. Just stay the course and you'll get there.

The last fifteen months have been indescribable. I feel so much better now than I ever could have imagined. I honestly didn't realize how poor my health was. Now that I know what feeling healthy feels like, I have no desire to ever destroy my body again. I have restored the temple; I have renovated God's creation. No longer am I a tenement in desperate need of repair. My life is no longer rundown.

I've lost 150 pounds, my waistline has shrunk from a size 48 to a 34, and my self-confidence and self-esteem have never been higher. I have a new lease on life. I have rededicated my life to God, to my family, and to my health. In his book *Wild at Heart*, John Eldredge said, "Life is not a problem to be solved; it is an adventure to be lived." Well, the adventure I've been on since October 2012 has certainly been the ride of my life.

Appendix A

Name	Normal	10/12/12	1/11/13	4/18/13	10/18/13
Glucose	70-120	210	115	102	102
A1C	4.8-5.6	7.9	5.8	5.4	5.4
AST (Liver)	0-40	77	31	22	15
ALT (Liver)	0-40	142	47	22	12
Cholesterol	100-199	231	221	163	174
Triglycerides	0-149	290	247	165	130
Testosterone	348-1197	65	-	94	-
Weight	-	377	328	292	243
Waistline	-	48	42	38	34

Appendix A

Appendix B

Sample of daily diet before 10/10/12

Breakfast
2 Pop Tarts
16 oz. Coffee w/4 TB of creamer
Calories: 520   Fat: 16   Carbohydrates: 87

Lunch
Bacon Cheeseburger
Large French Fries
Large Soft Drink
Cookie
Calories: 1570   Fat: 84   Carbohydrates: 169

Dinner
Large Serving of Pasta w/Meat Sauce
2-3 Pieces of Garlic Bread
12 oz. Soft Drink
Calories: 1050   Fat: 29   Carbohydrates: 170

Snacks
Large Bowl of Ice Cream
Half a Bag of Potato Chips
Calories: 730   Fat: 44   Carbohydrates: 79

Daily Totals
Calories: 3870   *Fat: 173*   *Carbohydrates: 505*

Sample of daily diet between 10/11/12 and 10/30/12

Breakfast
Large Banana
16 oz. Coffee w/4 TB of Sugar-Free Creamer
Calories: 170   Fat: 7   Carbohydrates: 35

Lunch
Turkey Sandwich on Wheat Bread w/Slice of Cheese
Calories: 270   Fat: 7   Carbohydrates: 35

Dinner
Baked Chicken
Salad w/Fat-Free Italian Dressing
Calories: 240   Fat: 4   Carbohydrates: 12

Snacks
Fiber Brownie
Calories: 90   Fat: 3   Carbohydrates: 18

Daily Totals
Calories: 770   Fat: 21   Carbohydrates: 100

Sample of daily diet after 10/30/12

Breakfast
Large Banana
Lean Pocket Breakfast Sandwich
16 oz. Coffee w/4 TB of Sugar-Free Creamer
Calories: 440   Fat: 14   Carbohydrates: 68

Lunch
Turkey Sandwich on Wheat Bread w/Slice of Cheese
Low-Fat Greek Yogurt
Calories: 370   Fat: 7   Carbohydrates: 49

Dinner
Taco Salad w/Venison and Low-Carb Tortilla (Baked)
1/2 Serving of Spanish Rice
Calories: 520   Fat: 20   Carbohydrates: 60

Snacks
Fiber Brownie
Serving of Almonds
Apple
Calories: 330   Fat: 17   Carbohydrates: 46

Daily Totals
Calories: 1660 Fat: 58 Carbohydrates: 223